WHAT IF YOU COULD

Also by

Jacinda Ardern

<<<

FOR ADULTS

A Different Kind of Power

>>>

FOR YOUNG READERS

Mom's Busy Work

JACINDA ARDERN

WHAT IF YOU COULD

ADAPTED FOR
YOUNG READERS BY
RUBY SHAMIR

PHILOMEL

PHILOMEL
An imprint of Penguin Random House LLC
1745 Broadway, New York, NY 10019
penguinrandomhouse.com

Edited by Talia Benamy

Text set in Minion Pro, Stylo Marker, Hearns, and Peperoncino Sans Crash

Library of Congress Cataloging-in-Publication Data is available.

First published in the United States of America by Philomel, 2026

Printed and bound by CPI Group (UK) Ltd, Croydon, CR0 4YY

ISBN 9780593692219

The authorized representative in the EU for product safety and compliance is Penguin Random House Ireland, Morrison Chambers, 32 Nassau Street, Dublin D02 YH68, Ireland, https://eu-contact.penguin.ie.

1

For the leaders of tomorrow—
who just don't know it yet

CONTENTS

WHAT IF YOU COULD

PROLOGUE

THERE ARE NOT a lot of options available to you when you are alone and stuck in a school bathroom stall after hours. There's the usual method of just opening the latch, but I had tried that for five minutes and all I had managed to do was take the skin off one finger. There's the option of shimmying under the door—but the gap for this particular stall was on the small side. Besides, I'd already weighed the risk and decided that being found wedged halfway under a bathroom stall door would be much more humiliating than the situation I was already in. I was at Cambridge High School, and the regional United Nations speech competition was about to start. But instead of warming up, I was stuck in a bathroom and starting to panic.

My nerves at speech competitions weren't the best under normal circumstances, even when I wasn't trapped in a restroom. While I loved talking to people to share a story or an idea, the worry that came with public speaking was almost debilitating. From the moment a competition was announced, I fixated on it, barely thinking of anything else. I slept poorly the night before each competition, waking up every few moments to work through whether I had memorized my speech well enough and what I would do if I lost my place. By morning, my stomach went into such terrible knots, I couldn't eat.

As my speeches grew longer, I discovered a new problem, the worst one of all: Sometimes I couldn't speak. Literally. It always happened about three or four minutes in: My mouth went bone dry. My lips began to stick against my teeth. I struggled to form words properly, and if the speech went more than five minutes, I'd be unable to say anything at all. The cause was simple: When I was nervous, I lost the ability to make any spit in my mouth. It was as if my brain was so focused on whatever was causing my stress to go up and my heart to race, it couldn't do anything else.

I tried everything to fix it—strong mints, drinking lemon water, repeating the word *lemon*, *lemon*, *lemon* before taking the stage. My mother even visited the pharmacist, returning with a set of candies intended for cancer patients whose salivary glands had been damaged. Nothing worked. If anything, my obsession made it even worse.

Interestingly, I never stopped to ask myself *why* I was so nervous. By all standard measures, I was good at giving speeches. I spent time preparing my arguments carefully. I learned every speech so thoroughly, I barely ever needed to glance at the index cards I made. I had won prizes at school and a few regional ones too. But the truth was, I could never shake the feeling that something could go terribly wrong. And that when it did, not only would I let people down, but it would also be proof that I wasn't good enough to be there in the first place.

It was my history teacher Mr. Fountain who came closest to explaining what was going on. He'd also done speech competitions in high school, even winning the national United Nations competition in 1989. When I told him about the extent of my nerves, he nodded thoughtfully. "You know, Jacinda," he said, "some days I stand up at the front of this classroom, convinced that someone is going to jump out from behind those desks and reveal to the whole room that I don't actually know what I'm doing." It took me a moment to understand what he was saying. Mr. Fountain was the best teacher I'd ever had. And yet, what he was describing felt so familiar. That's when he used a phrase I would remember for the rest of my life.

He said, "That feeling is called impostor syndrome."

I took this in. *Impostor syndrome.* Two words that felt like pieces of a puzzle clicking together. I could not imagine why Mr. Fountain would ever suffer from a problem like this, but I wasn't ready to give myself that same grace. *His* worry was irrational, I thought; *mine* was not. But still, there was so much comfort in this moment. If Mr. Fountain felt the way I did, if there were *two* of us, then other people probably felt it too. Probably many people did—after all, the phenomenon had a name.

By now, I had been in the bathroom stall for at least five minutes, my heart banging so hard in my chest that I felt it thumping in my throat. All I could think was: I'm going to miss the competition altogether. And that would mean letting everyone down: my school, my teachers, my mum.

I suddenly stopped. Stopped wriggling, stopped thinking, stopped silently praying. I stood still, breathed in, and placed my hands back on the lock to try to slide it one more time. The force ripped at the raw skin on my already bleeding finger as the lock sprung back. I was free. I was so relieved I wanted to cry. Instead I washed my hands in the sink and ran into the darkened hallway. The teacher who had pointed me in the direction of the bathroom was walking toward me.

"There you are, we'd wondered what had happened to you! Are you ready?"

No. I am not ready. I will never be ready. This will never get easier.

"Yup, ready to go!" I said as cheerfully as I could. "Let's do this."

On October 26, 2017, at the age of thirty-seven, I was sworn in as the fortieth prime minister of New Zealand. I never expected to become a politician, and certainly never dreamed I'd become prime minister, the head of our government. Not when I had always worried that I was never quite good enough. That at any moment I would be caught short, and that no matter *what* I was doing, I had no business doing it.

During high school I discovered a love of politics, because I saw it as the forum where I could use my skills, interests, and passions to solve big problems that society faced, problems that I cared deeply about: child poverty, homelessness, hunger, climate change, and more. I thought a lot about the way the government and laws could either support or get in the way of justice, fairness, equality, and human rights. But I also believed my personality was better suited to making a difference behind the scenes. I was the worker who quietly and steadily got things done. I wasn't tough enough to become an actual politician. My elbows weren't sharp enough; my skin was too thin. I was idealistic and sensitive.

But as time went on, a set of questions kept cropping up: What if my fear of failing, of letting people down, was overshadowed by a grinding sense of responsibility? What if these dueling impulses could push me forward, urging me to put aside those fears and instead practice, learn, and listen to others? What if my biggest weaknesses were actually strengths? Where might that lead? As it turned out: to some pretty exciting things.

PART ONE

1

What If You Could Listen

YOU COULD DRIVE for thirty miles in the Kāingaroa Forest and wonder if there's anything left on earth besides trees. That's the view: radiata pines, each standing one hundred feet tall, as far as the eye can see. The forest is as vast as it is dense: tree upon tree, row upon row, mile upon mile. The sameness is broken by only two things. First, the road carving through the shadowy landscape, and then the radiata shoots, popping up sporadically and defiantly. These smaller, wilding pines look like the Christmas trees of my childhood—joyful but a bit pathetic, each with just a few sparse branches, enough for only a single string of tinsel that will never quite hide the exposed trunk.

Although Kāingaroa is man-made—it's the second largest timber plantation in the southern hemisphere—it is easy to feel isolated there. It's a forest that has been known to swallow up hunters and hikers who get lost among the pines. Damp mists are common, and light struggles to break through, especially after the sun dips behind the green peaks of the distant Te Urewera mountain ranges. Needles and cones collect on the forest floor, and the air is thick with the scent of resin and pine.

But an hour into the journey, just as you become certain you've reached the middle of nowhere, there is a break in the trees, and signs of human life return: A run-down forestry building with a rusted sign. A timber motel with small, neat rooms. Then, around the corner, a service station with three gas pumps that marks the entry to a town called Murupara.

As a young girl, I made that trip through the forest countless times. Today, when I close my eyes, I can still take myself there: the twisting road that gives way to the long stretch of blacktop, the gray mass of the mountains, rough trunks piercing the sky.

The first time I visited Murupara in 1985, I was four years old and sick with the flu in the back seat of my family's Toyota Corona. In those days, I was also prone to car sickness, which was almost certainly made worse by my brown corduroy booster seat, little more than a wedge of dense foam covered in fabric. It gave me height, but it also exaggerated every turn in the road. Next to me sat my sister Louise, just eighteen months older than me, each of us clutching our teddy bears. She was also in a booster, and queasy, but not so much that she would stop asking questions of my parents: *How much longer? Why can't we stop? What if I need the toilet?*

The windows were rolled down just enough that I could hang my fingers over the top and wiggle them in the open air. Beneath my dangling feet were the items that my mum made sure accompanied us on every long car trip: an old towel and an empty, half-gallon plastic ice cream container, in case we needed to throw up. She never threw anything away, and even this container would likely later be repurposed to store home-baked blueberry muffins. Between me and Louise, trapped inside a carboard box with small holes at the top, sat the most uncomfortable passenger of all: our gray rescue cat, Norm. The sedative from the vet was wearing off as he pressed his face up against the top of the box, whiskers sticking out through the holes.

It was moving day. We had left behind friends and family in the city of Hamilton, more than two hours to the northwest, because my dad had just taken a new job, as the police sergeant in Murupara, a place I'd never seen.

Dad had grown up in a large family in Te Aroha, a farming community in the shadow of mountains along the Waihou River.

Like every region in New Zealand, Te Aroha was settled first by Māori, who'd navigated their way from Polynesia in waka (canoes) using stars, ocean swells, and sea life as their guides. These Māori tribes had lived on this land for hundreds of years before any European even knew it existed. Legend had it that the great chief Kahu climbed to the peak of a mountain to orient himself and was so moved to see his home from this vantage point that he named it Te Muri-aroha-o-Kahu, te aroha-tai, te aroha-uta, meaning "the love of Kahu for those on the coasts and those on the land." Now it's known simply as Mount Te Aroha, the mountain of love.

By the time my dad was born, the population of Te Aroha was majority *pākehā*, New Zealanders of European descent. My dad's family ran the local drain-laying business, and Ardern and Sons had dug most of the drains in the area. As a boy, my dad had helped out, but when his family converted to the Church of Jesus Christ of Latter-day Saints, or what many know as Mormonism, Dad left Te Aroha to attend the Mormon boarding school. There he set his sights on doing something other than laying drains. He joined the New Zealand Police at age nineteen, serving first as a uniformed officer in Auckland and then as a detective in Hamilton.

Dad was endlessly interested in people; he always wanted to know about their lives. As a police officer, he didn't simply want to know what crimes had been committed; he also wanted to know *why.* I would often hear him say that the police can't arrest their way out of everything. He believed if you wanted to fix crime, you had to understand why it was happening in the first place. This isn't to say he was soft. I doubt you could say that of anyone who investigated the brutal crimes my dad did: murder, robberies, and gang violence. He just looked at problems differently.

Policing is also different in New Zealand than in many countries. For one, officers don't routinely carry guns. And while they have the power to make arrests, they use a British principle known as "policing by consent." The idea is that police are essentially citizens in uniforms, and their authority stems from the approval and cooperation of the community. Although not everyone has always policed with this approach—and there have been examples of abuse of power in New Zealand's police force—policing by consent is the model that officers are expected to follow, and it was what my dad believed in.

Dad was an excellent detective. He asked good questions, and people talked to him, sometimes sharing personal details. It wasn't unusual for someone my father was questioning to pause and observe, "At least you're listening to me."

I remember as a young university student, sitting with Dad in a booth at Burger King in Hamilton. My back was to the counter when I looked up from my Whopper to see my dad lock eyes with someone he recognized. I flicked my head around in time to see a solidly built man lifting his eyebrows and nodding his head at Dad—a greeting in New Zealand we call the "east coast wave." Dad did the same in return.

"Who's that?" I asked, assuming it was likely someone he went to school with.

My dad started to unwrap his burger, and casually, he said, "Just a man I've arrested a few times." Dad's approach made an imprint on me, though I had no idea then that listening to people tell stories about their struggles and their lives would wind up being a big part of my own.

Dad enjoyed the work in Hamilton, but he wanted to run a station rather than just work in one. So, when I was a toddler, he began studying for his sergeant's exams, which was no small effort. He already had a full-time job and a young family, and he was active in the Mormon church. To prepare, he rose before dawn, getting in an hour or two of study before the rest of us woke up. Then he would study again after dark.

But even when Dad passed all his exams, there was still the issue of finding a place that needed to hire a sergeant. Sergeant jobs were scarce and competitive, and without leadership experience, it would be near impossible for him to be promoted in Hamilton or a similar station elsewhere. That meant one thing: going somewhere almost no one else wanted to go.

So, there we were, arriving in Murupara as a family for the first time: my parents in the front seat, two queasy girls in the back, and a gray cat in a box desperate to be liberated.

The forest surrounding Murupara felt towering, but the small town itself was low and open, the buildings there flat and simple. And while many streets were named after trees—Kauri, Rimu, Pūriri—there were very few trees lining them. It was a forestry town with no forest of its own.

Our new home was on Kōwhai Avenue, named for a small, woody tree with bursts of bright yellow flowers in spring (the word *kōwhai* means *yellow* in Māori). The house was a solid rectangle of cream brick, plain and practical, with a small, corrugated iron garage on one side. There was no garden, just a concrete path that led to the front door. But from almost the moment the moving trucks arrived, my mother set out to make a home for us, hanging curtains and planting pansies in the yard. Every morning, Mum breezed into my and Louise's bedroom, pulling back the curtains she'd hung, declaring "Wakey, wakey!" Mum was a "potterer," constantly scrubbing, wiping, sorting, all the while narrating to herself what she was doing and what she planned to take on next.

The house was small, with two bedrooms. First was the small one that Louise and I shared, with barely enough room for two single beds and a small set of drawers (but still large enough for Louise to declare "her" side the tidy one). My parents' bedroom was slightly larger, able to fit a queen-sized bed and a few pieces of furniture. Down the narrow hall was a third room where my mother hand-sewed clothes and folded endless piles of laundry. The living room had a simple fireplace that in winter stayed burning through the night to warm the house. The kitchen was purely functional, with pink wooden cabinets, metal handles, and a stainless steel counter.

In this modest space, my parents arranged their most cherished possessions: a pine-framed sofa with hard wooden arms and scratchy plaid cushions. Mum and Dad's wedding photo, set in an ornate gold frame. A set of matte brown Crown Lynn dinnerware, a wedding present that Mum decreed could be used on only special occasions (and as a result mostly sat on display in a cabinet). An old-fashioned tube TV with a built-in speaker, woven and green. On top of that television, they placed our newest possession: a bulky silver Panasonic VCR, which had cost my parents the equivalent of a month's salary. I knew this because we were reminded of its cost almost every time it was used.

What our new house lacked in space it made up for in an enormous, wide-open backyard. The yard was large enough for a trampoline, as well as a rotary clothesline that my sister and I circled as we learned to ride our bikes. If Louise and I jumped on the trampoline high enough, we could just see the blue roof of the police station come in and out of view.

Next door to us lived my dad's co-worker Hamish with his wife, Joan. I have almost no memory of Joan, other than her warmth. Hamish was roughly the same age as my dad, lean with a thinning crop of golden hair. There was one other officer posted to the station, and between him, Hamish and my father, they made up the entirety of the Murupara police force. These three officers covered not only the town of Murupara, but also the large, rural, and remote surrounding areas. Backup reinforcements, if needed, were almost an hour away.

On the face of it, Murupara was a hard town. And there were reasons for this, some dating back hundreds of years.

In the years before our arrival in Murupara, more than half of the town's forestry workforce had lost their jobs due to government reforms that had changed New Zealand's economy dramatically. Many of those who could leave, did. Businesses shuttered, and many families fell further into poverty.

This wasn't the first blow to this small town. Māori, who made up most of the town, were already carrying the scars of colonization. In 1642, Dutch explorer Abel Tasman first laid eyes on the land we now know as Aotearoa, New Zealand—

the land of the long white cloud. Next came James Cook, followed by whalers, traders, Christian missionaries, and settlers. These waves of newcomers had often brutal results for tangata whenua, the people of the land, including land confiscation, warfare, and loss of lives, income, and mana—dignity. The economic changes intensified this history.

By the time we arrived in Murupara, it seemed that some of the most well-off people in town were members of local gangs: the Mongrel Mob or the Tribesmen. One gang was headquartered in a nearby town, the other in Murupara with a large, corrugated iron fence surrounding the gang "pad," high enough that you couldn't see the house behind it.

I often heard the gang members in town well before I saw them, the roar of their high-handled motorbikes so loud that Louise sometimes stopped walking to cover her ears. If the bikes passed by school, kids ran to the window to watch. After all, no one had motorbikes like the gang members.

It was in Murupara that I went to school for the first time. I wasn't quite five years old, but the school suggested that there was little point in waiting for my birthday, that I might as well begin kindergarten as Louise entered second grade. It was deep in winter the day we started, and the two of us held hands as we set off walking together.

That first morning, the teacher called out the roll alphabetically. My last name put me at the top of the list, and as my name was called, I sat up on the mat, legs crossed in front of me, and yelled back "Yes!" enthusiastically. As the teacher continued to call the roll, other kids offered a different reply: "Āe," the Māori word for *yes*. I noted this, that's all. I had grown up with Māori words used interchangeably with English—words like *European*, *stomach*, *family*, and *love* were frequently switched out with *pākehā*, *puku*, *whānau*, and *aroha*.

I had Māori relatives on both sides of my family, and we were Mormon, and in New Zealand Māori made up much of the membership of Mormon churches. But this was the first time I was surrounded by children who spoke te reo, the Māori language, so freely and openly.

Today, I know that I was on the land of the Ngāti Manawa people, the Māori tribe of the area. In decades past, there had been repeated conflict on their land leading to the loss of crops, the government had broken lease agreements, and disease had taken the lives of many.

At five, I knew none of this. I simply noticed the words, the same way I noted other things: That the school grounds were enormous, big enough to play large games of tag. That we had mat time and stories. That on Fridays, we were allowed to order fish and chips, which came in tightly wrapped newspaper that we'd rip the top off of to dig into the steaming fries. That the other kids liked to go barefoot in summer like I did—sometimes even to school.

Not long after we started school, Louise and I were walking home together when we heard crying. It was a small boy—smaller even than I was. He was just across the street, his back to us. He was alone. It was cold by now, the kind of cold when snow settled on the mountain ranges and ice hardened on the tops of puddles. It was the kind of cold that gets into your bones, but this boy was wearing shorts, and his feet were bare. He carried a giant backpack, which dwarfed him completely. From beneath his shorts, brown streaks, diarrhea, ran down the backs of his legs.

My sister and I slowed down. The boy's sobs were loud and sounded a bit like choking. I was still so young, but I was old enough to have a persistent thought. *He shouldn't be alone.* My sister and I held hands and watched him silently. I think we both believed it was better if he didn't know we'd seen him. We watched him move farther from us, and all the while I willed, as hard as I could, but silently: *Please. Someone come and find him.*

Murupara was small enough that Louise and I were allowed to walk by ourselves to the small set of shops in the center of town, less than a five-minute walk if we cut through the back of the police station. The local security guard assigned to keep watch over the shops would sometimes be parked in the middle of the parking lot, dozing in his car. Other times flatbed pickup trucks with the large carcass of a wild pig or a deer would be idling nearby, ready to do another victory lap of town before being taken home to be skinned and carved up.

Among the stores was a pharmacy, a post office, a butcher, Four Square (a miniature supermarket), just one fish-and-chip shop, and a corner dairy. Dairies are like very small convenience stores with a little bit of everything, including candy. There, we'd approach the counter with coins. For twenty cents, we could buy a white paper bag twisted at the top full of chewy Milk Bottles, fizzy candies, and gummies in the shape of jet planes.

Getting to and from the dairy took you past the Murupara Hotel, which wasn't a hotel at all but a pub. It was a plain white building with a faded green roof and slatted windows that revealed nothing of the inside. Anyone and everyone went to the Hotel. When it closed for the evening, the hardier patrons often didn't go home. Instead, they gathered out back, where they continued drinking long into the night.

When our family needed groceries, we'd climb into the Toyota Corona to make an hour-long journey to the Pak 'n Save in Rotorua. Back we'd head, through that deep, dark forest, until the fragrance of pine gave way to the sulfuric smell of Rotorua's hot springs. One Saturday, my car sickness got the better of me, and I threw up on my clothes. The remainder of that drive was spent with the windows down while my mum cursed not bringing an ice cream container. When we arrived in Rotorua, my father drove me to the police station, where he hosed me off—literally—as my mum picked up a brand-new outfit. I remember it exactly: a pale green floral skirt with an embroidered trim, and a matching blouse with a round collar. It was one of the few outfits I owned in those days that was neither hand-sewn nor a hand-me-down. After that bonus outfit, I dreaded the feeling of car sickness a little less.

Despite the winding roads, Louise and I looked forward to our Saturday trips to Rotorua, especially in the early days when we didn't have many friends. The other kids in school were understandably wary of us. We weren't just the new kids, the outsiders, we were the daughters of the police sergeant, the man who locked people up. Louise bore the brunt of this suspicion. She was called names and teased, so I began following her around at lunchtime like a self-appointed protector.

It would be years before I'd understand that in Murupara, there was long-standing distrust of the state in all sorts of ways.

But even as a child, I had some sense that the police were especially mistrusted, and I suppose I could even understand why. Police didn't just arrest criminals—nameless, faceless bad guys. They arrested people in the community: dads, brothers, sisters, aunties, and mums. If a child's parent was arrested, there was a very good chance my dad would have had something to do with it. I tried to imagine how that must feel: Someone in a uniform shows up at the door and then your family member is taken away. *But they don't know my dad*, I'd tell myself. I was convinced that if they did, things would get better.

Perhaps that's why Dad had wanted to run his own station in the first place. Since becoming a police officer, he'd noticed many moments when a parent, upon seeing him in uniform, would lean down to a child and whisper a warning of some sort. *See that police officer over there? If you're naughty, he's going to come and arrest you.* Dad would tell me how much he hated hearing kids be told that. He wanted people to believe that their lives were better because the police were there. But that kind of policing takes trust, and trust takes time.

One day, I headed into town, cutting from the backyard into the police station parking lot. There, I saw a group of men in leather pants and jackets gathered around a figure in a blue uniform:

my dad. He was shorter than the men who surrounded him, and he was alone. The men moved around him slowly, menacingly, kicking up loose gravel as they moved. Even from a distance I could see Dad's body was tense; he held up one arm in front of himself, as if trying to both keep the men calm and keep them at a distance. Even though I was too small to understand all that was happening, I knew the situation wasn't good.

I didn't want my dad to see me, but turning around and going back seemed just as likely to catch Dad's eye as trying to skirt past. So I kept going, approaching in a near-tiptoe, placing one bare foot in front of the other, trying to make myself as small as possible. But I couldn't keep my eyes off what was happening. Dad's eyes locked onto mine. I froze.

When my father spoke, his voice was slow and calm.

"Keep walking, Jacinda," he said.

I did, moving as quickly as my bare feet allowed on the painful gravel scattered over the driveway. When I reached the concrete sidewalk, I broke into a run. But I worried about my dad, so much that I risked his annoyance and took the same route to return home. By now, the parking lot was empty.

That night, when Dad came home, I asked him how he got out of the situation. I couldn't imagine an exit other than force. I must have said something like this, because he furrowed his brow, his expression making it clear that he was disappointed in me.

"Jacinda," he said. "My words will always be the greatest tool I have."

Words as a tool—for talking and for listening, for reasoning and for understanding, for building trust. Dad's explanation stuck with me for the rest of my life.

2

What If You Could Find Your Purpose

SEVERAL MONTHS AFTER we moved to Murupara, there was a fight on the lawn that stretched between our home and Hamish's. Roughly twenty men spilled out from a nearby party, drunk and swearing, throwing messy punches at one another as my mother watched from the kitchen window. Brawls like this weren't unheard of, and they tended to end pretty quickly. But this one kept going. At one point, the men turned from each other to a sudden awareness of where they were.

"Let's smash the sergeant's windows!" one of them shouted.

The windows closest to them were the same ones under which my sister and I were sleeping. My mother made a quick calculation. Should she wake us up and move us, or leave us to sleep? She decided to spare Louise and me from the panic of a late-night wake-up, instead turning to the best protection she could imagine: She prayed.

My mother was raised Presbyterian, one of five children of conservative farmers on a 144-acre dairy farm in rural Waikato, where the nearest small town was five miles away. Life on the farm was hard. My grandparents rose at five a.m. to prepare for the first milking of the day; the work often continued past nightfall. My grandfather Eric was a direct man. If you made a mistake, or did something clumsy or thoughtless, he'd sigh with indignation, then correct you sharply. There was just too much to do to waste time on mistakes. My grandmother Margaret was similarly practical, the type of woman who placed her small kids in a playpen next to the shed while she got the milking done.

Growing up, Mum worked hard: first on the farm, then at a service station doing bookkeeping, and finally at the post office in Te Aroha. That's what she was doing when she met my dad, not the first guy she'd dated, but the one she set her sights on marrying.

Dad rode a motorcycle and wore his hair long at the back, with flared jeans and plaid shirts. But he opened the car door for my mum, and as a Mormon, he didn't drink alcohol, which for my mother was a relief. Dad never tried to convert my mother. But after they started dating, Mum took a holiday to the Gold Coast of Australia, where she met Mormon missionaries and read the Book of Mormon for the first time. Something clicked. She liked the doctrine, the direct and personal relationship members had with God, the focus on service and the care of others. For her, it felt like truth. She did not need her parents' blessing to convert, nor did she get it. My grandparents were Baptists now, and they didn't see Mormonism as a real religion. Despite her parents' objections, my mother was baptized Mormon and married in the Mormon church.

Which is how she found herself praying as a drunken mob considered smashing the windows beneath which her daughters slept. Whether it was divine intervention or simply good police training, my father and Hamish arrived and eventually managed to disperse the mass of people, and our windows stayed intact. Soon after, the police installed a fence in front of our house.

But in many ways, our home was always just an extension of the police station. When the station was closed, people came to our house. My mum's diary from those days is a testament to nonstop visits and phone calls. One night my dad finished work at six p.m. Then there were knocks at the door at nine p.m., and then again at ten p.m. At eleven thirty p.m. the phone rang; a man had been run over by two young people while walking down a local road. My dad returned home from that incident at three a.m. He was just climbing into bed when someone from our local church pounded on the door. The man's car had been stolen with his tools inside, and he wanted my father's help to search for them. My father helped him look until five thirty in the morning. Dad had been in bed for just an hour when the doorbell rang again, the start of a whole new day. This constant disruption wasn't unusual. One day, annoyed at the doorbell's constant chime, my mother threatened to smash it with a hammer.

My mother was also cautious about bothering my dad. Extremely cautious. One night, I found my father's handcuffs and managed to lock myself in them. My mother couldn't find the key anywhere in the house. So, even though Dad was right next door at the station, I sat with those heavy cuffs around my wrists learning a lesson until he returned home.

All this activity was hard on Mum. She was just twenty-nine years old when we moved to Murupara and was busy looking after two young children. Her family was far away, and Dad was always working. Even her paid job didn't offer much of a break. When Dad came home, she would head over to the police station to clean it on her own, earning $4.18 an hour.

Meanwhile, Louise struggled at school. She was tall for her age, but she was also lean, and shier than I was. One day I was home sick when Louise, still just six years old, arrived at the end of the day crying. She told my mother that a group of boys had pinned her down and sat on her, hitting her on her head and body.

Mum had known that Louise was having trouble making friends, and that sometimes kids gave us a hard time. But until that afternoon, she hadn't known that I'd been following my sister around the playground, or that things were dire enough that Louise might be physically hurt. That was too much for her.

My mother drove to a neighboring school eight miles outside of town and asked them to enroll us. The principal refused. My mother waited a week, then returned, and asked again. Perhaps the principal had a change of heart. Or maybe he realized that my mother would persist until he agreed. So, he relented. After this, each morning at seven forty-five a.m., Louise and I boarded a school bus in front of the Murupara Hotel and took the thirty-minute trip to school in Galatea.

In my mother's diary from the early days of Murupara, there's a matter-of-fact entry. Dad had been dispatched to make an arrest in a nearby settlement, and when he returned his uniform was torn. When Mum asked what happened, his answer was suspiciously brief. She understood by what he didn't say that in the process of making the arrest, he'd been attacked. This diary entry is notable for how unemotional it is. Mum was relaying facts, that's all.

But soon after, Mum describes having trouble breathing. It is clear to me today, reading these diary pages, that she had started having panic attacks. But this was the 1980s, long before words like *panic attack* became commonplace. And even then, there were no long descriptions, no complaints about how difficult she was finding things. Just a note that she had moments when she could not breathe.

Mum remained stoic and optimistic. That is, right up until the moment she couldn't.

For the most part, I have almost no memory of my mother struggling. She worked hard to hide it from us. Her diary records that when we would drive back toward Murupara after getting the groceries, there was a turnoff where without fail she would begin to cry silently. But she was determined that my sister and I would not see her.

On one occasion, though, I did see. Mum and I were home alone. I walked into the kitchen and found her leaning against the kitchen counter. She didn't turn toward me as she usually might, didn't ask what I needed in the way that my mother did as a matter of habit for everyone she loved and cared for. Mum didn't seem to register that I was there. She wasn't pottering or fussing, making scones or preparing lunch.

Her back was to me, apron strings tied around her middle. Both hands were pressed up against the edge of the stainless steel counter; one clutched a tea towel so hard it looked as if it should have been giving her something in exchange for her force. She rocked back and forth ever so slightly. I didn't need to see her face to know she was crying.

I wanted her to know that I was there. I thought that might break her from this spell. I came up alongside her leg. But as I reached her, she turned on her heels and headed to the back door. Tea towel still in hand, she disappeared through the doorway.

I stared after her. Then I followed, half running to catch up. But my short legs couldn't keep up with her stride. I watched her move away from me, confusion and fear rising inside my chest. I wanted to know that she was okay. I also didn't want to be alone. I was too little to be alone.

Mum crossed the yard to the gate that connected our property to Hamish's. Then she disappeared for a second time. By the time I reached Hamish's back door and entered the kitchen, my mother was sitting at the kitchen table, head bowed into her tea towel. Joan was next to her. When I remember this moment today, I cannot see Joan's face. I remember her more as a presence—legs standing next to Mum, one hand on Mum's shoulder. Joan had always been kind to me and Louise. But when she turned away from Mum and toward me, she was focused and serious.

"Go home, Jacinda," she said. Her voice was clear and firm.

But my home is here, I thought. *My mother is here.*

I don't really recall the days that followed. I do know my mum was home with us, but she tells me now that she spent most of that time in bed. Nobody explained much. I'm not sure a nervous breakdown can be adequately explained to a child as young as I was. But I understand now what happened.

I also understand that my father did what he could to help. He would come home from his shift at work and make meals or do ironing and help us tidy our room. He took us all to the beach at Mount Maunganui for a break, and apparently it helped.

But when we returned, those same silent tears that always plagued Mum came again. After the trip my mother wrote in her diary that she was feeling "unwell again." The next morning, she got herself up long enough to get my sister and me off to school and then crawled back into bed.

Six weeks later, Hamish and Joan finished their allotted time in Murupara and prepared to return to their home in Nelson. My mother made them their last evening meal, and then, the next morning, as the movers loaded their possessions into the truck, she fed them breakfast. She recorded this in her diary, noting that my father planned to talk to his supervisor because she was "getting no better."

As she wrote those words, she had two and a half more years in Murupara in front of her.

In the end, I think three things helped Mum keep going: her faith, her church community, and trout fishing.

There are several rivers near Murupara, and somewhere along the line, Mum decided that she was going to teach herself to catch trout. The hobby provided both a mini-getaway and perhaps a way of taking back some control over life. She'd grab her pole, pack me and Louise reluctantly into the car, and head out to the middle of nowhere. I can still picture her standing on the edge of the rushing water in her giant glasses; bright green gym shorts, the kind with the white piping at the edges; a tight T-shirt on top. She'd stand there for hours, absolutely focused. Meanwhile, Louise and I hung out on the banks, bored out of our minds. We played with sticks and made up imaginary games until we couldn't take it anymore.

"Muuuuum . . ." we would whine. "Can we go home?"

Mum would quietly cast again.

"Mummmm, we need to go to the toilet!"

Keeping her eyes fixed on the water, she'd respond impatiently, "Well, go and find a tree." Eventually that was what we'd do.

Sometimes people offered to help her fish. She might take the odd lesson or their advice about new spots to try. But I think Mum preferred to be out there alone, stubbornly mastering this new skill. She could cast; I watched her do it countless times. But I recall only one fish being caught. It wasn't large, but it was big enough for Dad to smoke it in the backyard and for us to all tell Mum how delicious her hard-earned fish was.

Mum was also committed to Murupara's Mormon church, as she was to every church we attended. In Murupara, services were held in a classroom at the local elementary school, with only a handful of members attending each week. But a nice thing about the Mormon church is that wherever you meet—whether in a makeshift hall or a brand-new chapel—you are welcome.

For three hours every Sunday, we gathered in that classroom for services, lessons, and activities. I remember almost nothing of the services we attended in Murupara, but I do remember many of the people. We got to know the handful of other church members, and Mum went out of her way to help everyone who needed it. There was the couple who had just bought a house when they separated. Mum helped them get their affairs in order, especially the wife, who found herself a single mum with two children, another on the way. Mum visited her often, putting her bookkeeping skills to use and helping with budgeting and whatever else she might need. When the baby arrived, Mum visited her at the hospital. I remember watching from the doorway as Mum wrapped her arms around this woman and her face lit up. They were, I now recognize, two women who needed one another.

Mum had found purpose: serving her community, a deep well into which she could pour her nurturing and from which she could draw strength and confidence. It was a lesson I would remember.

At church in Murupara, I made my own friend too: Walter, a sweet boy around my own age. He was thin and delicate, with dark hair and enormous brown eyes. Even at five, Walter was a gentle old soul—the kind of huge-hearted person who found the wonder in everything. Walter came to our home often. For hours, we'd sit on the floor—Walter, Louise, and I—playing dolls or dressing up. When the church put on a children's play, my mum made us costumes. I was Little Red Riding Hood and Walter played the wolf, but I could see that he longed for my red cape.

Sometimes Walter brought over his collection of cards. While many kids our age liked to collect things like wrestling cards, Walter collected the cards that accompanied sample perfume bottles—each scented with a spritz of fragrance. Walter glued the cards into an old school workbook, and we'd flip through them together, Walter pointing to his favorites or using them to pretend we worked at a pharmacy, as I pulled the book to my face, trying to discern any remaining scent of wildflowers or vanilla. Often, I smelled nothing at all. But I pretended I did. What mattered more than the scent was Walter's face of pure joy as we pored over these precious cards.

Dad, too, was making headway, working hard to be everywhere he was needed. People had begun to trust him a little more too. Once, he was in town when he spotted a gang member who was the subject of an arrest warrant. Dad approached him, ready to take him into his custody and escort him to the station several hundred feet away. The man surveyed his surroundings, including several of his associates nearby. Then he leaned into my dad.

"Is there another way to do this?" the man murmured.

My father looked around, saw the others watching. Dad realized that while the man had accepted his fate, he was looking for a shred of dignity in the situation. "I can arrest you here," my father told him quietly, "or in the next five minutes, you can walk yourself to the station." My dad left, and five minutes later, the gang member voluntarily walked into the station to be processed.

This approach didn't always produce the same result. Another time, my father was in a small nearby settlement of only a few hundred people called Ruatāhuna to talk to someone who had been growing large illegal drug crops. It was an hour-long drive back to the Murupara station, so my father asked the man to come in the next time he was in town.

The man instead decided to "go bush," heading for a hut deep into the forest. My father is kind but also firm. If you don't follow through, he will. On my mother's thirty-first birthday, Dad got up at six a.m., took his backpack, and headed out the door. He made the four-hour hike on the outskirts of Ruatāhuna, crossing a deep river eight times, before arriving at the man's hut.

The man greeted him with a defeated look. "I've been worried about you showing up," he sighed.

A year or so into our time in Murupara, my father volunteered himself for the dunk tank at the local school fair. The weather was cold; in the photos from that day, many people are wearing sweatshirts and jackets. One of the photos is of Dad, perched on a flimsy wooden plank above a tank of freezing water. His feet are bare, but he's otherwise in full uniform. He's smiling gamely, hands on his thighs, but his fingers are spread wide, as if he's preparing for the moment someone hits the target with a ball, releasing him into the water below. Surrounding him are people from town—children, parents, teachers—each ready to take their turn sending the police chief into the drink.

In the next photo, Dad's soaked, clearly still recovering after the shock of one of his many plunges. Around him, people are laughing. My mother is not in the frame, but I know she was right there, just out of view of the camera, smiling at Dad with a dry towel and spare set of clothes.

There's also a photo of me and Louise from one of these school fairs. We're in the back of a trailer—a hayride, I think. In the image, I'm standing up straight in a red sweater with a bright red jacket over the top, both of which make my blond mullet stand out. Next to me Louise is crouched down, peeking awkwardly over the edge of the trailer as if she is waiting for the tractor to lurch forward. Around us are other kids of all ages. One, a boy of about twelve in plaid flannel, waves happily at the person capturing the image. Another sucks on his finger while waving the other hand in the air. Several girls line the front of the trailer, their backs to the camera while they brace themselves for the ride. Looking at the image today, I'm aware of things that I don't remember noticing then—like the gang signals that some of the children are making, and that the only pākehā faces in that trailer are mine and Louise's. Back then though, we were just a bunch of kids. Some of us liked rugby or tag. Almost all of us liked candy, fish and chips, and sausage sizzles. Some didn't have shoes, and some may have lived in homes with broken windows, but all of us enjoyed a trailer ride at the local school fair.

At the beginning of 1988, having spent almost three years in the little house behind the police station, my family packed up the Toyota Corona again as a large truck reversed into our front yard to load up the Crown Lynn dinner set and our scratchy wooden couch. By this point, I had spent almost half my life in Murupara, but Dad had a new job.

As an adult, when people ask me where I'm from, Murupara is not the answer I give. But two decades later, when I was a newly elected member of the New Zealand parliament sitting in my office, a journalist asked me a different question. Our two chairs were facing each other, a notepad balanced on the journalist's lap with one arm extended, clutching a voice recorder.

"So," she asked me, "when did you first become political?"

I tapped my fingers across my lap, looking at her and then at the recorder. Behind her sat a large wooden bookcase full of blue-bound copies of legislation. My desk with its green leather inlay and tall reclining chair backed onto a view of the parliamentary atrium.

Just for a moment, I glanced at the bright light of the lamp sitting in the corner and thought about a different place entirely. I pictured a row of houses with wide open streets. I saw the sun bouncing off the black mat of a trampoline, bare feet skipping over the cracks in the pavement, stacks of twenty-cent candy bags. I saw a small boy clutching his book of perfume cards, and another dwarfed by his bag, walking and crying alone. I thought about fairness, and the way circumstances can push a community into difficulty—and the way the people in that community still managed to hang on to their mana, their dignity. I thought about my parents—about my dad, doing his best to help more than he hurt, and about my mum, doing her best to help others and to help herself too. And I knew: The answer was Murupara.

I became political because I lived in Murupara, a place that helped shape my own sense of purpose.

3

What If You Could Be Useful

I HAVE A DISTINCTIVE facial feature, and it's not what polite company would refer to as my broad smile. If you were to stand on my left, you wouldn't miss it: a thin white scar that begins at the inner corner of my eye, then follows the seam of my nose diagonally, all the way to the outer edge of my nostril. The scar is a permanent testament to my almost constant compulsion to be useful. It is also a physical memento of the small, three-acre orchard at the outskirts of a dairy farming town called Morrinsville, the place that I will forever call home.

I first got to know the orchard when my mum's parents, Granddad Eric and Grandma Margaret, owned it. The orchard was my grandparents' latest attempt at a new venture after they'd sold the dairy farm they'd owned and labored on for thirty years.

My granddad Eric, a towering man with sharp features, was as impatient as he was focused. He was always engaged in some sort of project: repairing, harvesting, tinkering, *improving*, often in his signature woolen shorts and socks pulled up to his knees. He was a man on a constant, unrelenting mission. When we visited the orchard, I sometimes peeked into the garage and watched as he talked to himself while he worked, just like my mother always did. *Right then*, he might say to himself as he moved through tasks. *Pop this here, and then this goes here.* Sometimes he hummed or sang a ditty. Either would bring a rare lightness to his face, which was otherwise, in those days, almost always stern.

Dad once told me that Granddad Eric was the smartest person he'd ever met. Everywhere I looked on that orchard there was evidence of Granddad's cleverness—the patched-up apple grader to sort the fruit, the bright red tractor he'd restored, old photos of boats he had built by hand. He'd built entire homes before too, but this one on the orchard—a creaky, two-story timber-framed structure—he'd altered and finished.

All Granddad's busyness meant he had little tolerance for mistakes, even from young children. So, Louise and I "helped" Grandma instead. I cannot remember a time that I saw Grandma Margaret wearing anything but a long skirt and blouse, her hair short and wavy, a slightly wilder version of the style worn by Queen Elizabeth of England, who, because of New Zealand's history and ties to the United Kingdom, was our head of state. Grandma Margaret's hair faded in color through the years, from the bright orange that shone in photos of her middle age to the grayish-white that I knew, but the style never changed.

Sometimes she plopped me and Louise into a trailer my granddad had built, hooked behind a riding lawn mower, and hauled us around the orchard. We sat there on hard wood, bumping and lurching next to trays of fruit, looking at the back of Grandma Margaret's head while her corgi, Shannon, trotted along beside us.

Every so often, Grandma Margaret turned around to check we weren't leaning too close to the edge of the trailer, flashing a smile of perfectly white false teeth before returning her gaze back to the sandy driveway. She was quick to laugh, and when she did, she threw her head back. Sometimes during those big belly laughs, her false teeth dropped away from her gums and reminded me of the chewy teeth we'd get in the candy mix at the corner store.

Often Louise and I played on our own at the orchard, running barefoot up and down through the rows of trees, careful to dodge bees hovering over the fruit on the ground. Whenever we stopped to catch our breath, we inhaled the sweet and sickly smell of rotting apples. But I didn't want to just play in the orchard. I wanted to *help*. I longed to wear a picking apron, to sort the fruit on the grader, or to operate the old red cherry picker to see if it could grab the apples that I couldn't reach by leaping into the air or standing on my tippy-toes.

These weren't jobs for a child, I was told. But sometimes my desire to help was bigger than my desire to be good, and on one visit I left the grown-ups talking by the house and snuck off to the quiet of the cool, damp packing sheds. That day, a piece of equipment Granddad used to make boxes sat near the fruit grader. It was even taller than he was, and it resembled a Ferris wheel. A wheel was for spinning, obviously, so I reached up to the cold metal and gave it a whirl. But I misjudged how close I could get—and how sharp the rough metal edges were. I felt pressure against my face and a stab of pain. Something wet trickled down my cheek.

By the time I stumbled into the bright light of the day and into the view of adults, my hands and face glistened with blood. The stitches I got that afternoon would become my scar, earned in a place that I loved and that I would soon call home. It also became an ever-present reminder that my constant drive to be useful could sometimes land me in trouble.

When Granddad Eric sold the family dairy farm, he moved into kiwifruit, then to Asian pears, and by 1988, around the time we were leaving Murupara, he had set his restless eye on the *next* big thing: avocados in Tauranga. My dad had his new job, a promotion to detective sergeant in nearby Hamilton. My parents were looking for a home, and Granddad was looking to sell. My grandparents sold the orchard to my parents. For my mum and dad, buying the orchard was a financial stretch and a risk. For me, the orchard felt at once like coming home *and* like a grand adventure.

Where Murupara was isolated and dominated by forestry, Morrinsville (with its population of roughly five thousand) was a dairy farming community, just twenty-five minutes to the nearest city of Hamilton and an hour from the beach. In fact, the official town motto would one day be "Morrinsville: Where You're Not Far from Anywhere"—a slogan that was dropped when officials realized it wasn't promoting coming to Morrinsville, but rather the convenience of leaving.

Morrinsville was the sort of town where people were split into two types: farmers and townies. Both groups were pragmatic, unpretentious, good-humored, and generally conservative. Townie and farmer alike could help you change the oil in your car as efficiently as they could milk a cow. When I was a kid, the only difference I saw between the two was that one got up earlier, wore farm boots, and drove farther to get groceries than the other. But even then, I knew it was intended as an insult if anyone ever called me a "townie."

Our house, with its two stories, was significantly bigger

than the one we'd had in Murupara, and spacious enough that Louise and I each had our own bedroom. It stood at the edge of town, adjacent to a cornfield and the Morrinsville Golf Course. For the entirety of our lives there, I heard dull thuds on the roof, or thwacks on the glass of windows, telling me that some novice golfer had just teed off.

To the west was a small forest about three acres in size. There wasn't much to this land, just some pine trees and a bit of undergrowth. But to me and Louise it was a mystery to be explored. In the forest, tree stumps became imaginary people, complete with backstories, occupying a world that was mine and Louise's alone.

When we weren't playing in the forest, Louise and I did jobs on the orchard. The task my parents had taken on by moving to a working orchard was monumental, and by now we were old enough to lend a hand without being a complete nuisance. Dad spent his days solving cases and making arrests. Then, in the evening, he'd walk through the door in a white shirt and dress pants, change into a pair of shorts and an old shirt, pull on his farm boots that had worn the hair off around his calf muscles, and head back outside. Sometimes I'd jump on my bike and pedal behind him, watching as he entered the shed, strapped the chemical sprayer on his back, and moved through the rows of trees spraying pesticide.

Louise and I weren't the most productive workers. The

apple-picking aprons hung to our knees, and if we filled them, they quickly became too heavy for us to lift over the apple bins. I tried to prune trees, but my hands weren't strong enough for the clippers. I packed boxes but struggled to lift them onto the pallets. There would be more jobs like this in the decades to come, jobs that would seem similarly unmanageable, where my attempts to be useful would feel like an unending uphill climb, where I'd maybe achieve only the most minuscule progress, or none at all. But even then, I would just keep going.

On the orchard, I probably got in the way more than I helped, just as I had with Granddad, but I would still put on my gray boots and race out with my headband slipping down over my eyes. All because I could see it and feel it: Mum and Dad needed help.

Five months after we arrived in Morrinsville, my uncle Mark, Mum's younger brother, was in a terrible car accident in a neighboring city. Mum told us he'd survived, but the doctors weren't sure his brain was alive. I thought about that a lot in the days after it happened: that a person can have a body that is breathing—they can be alive—without actually *being there.* My seven-year-old mind couldn't comprehend it. I wondered what it would mean if the doctors were wrong. If my uncle could hear us, and had been trying to speak but was frozen, the way I sometimes felt immobilized in nightmares. How frightening that would be.

Mum went back and forth to the hospital, and I peppered her with questions. Was he awake yet? Was he getting better? Could they test his brain to see if he was in there? Could they know for sure? I needed to see him for myself, but I was also afraid. Eventually, one day when Mum couldn't find someone to stay with us at home, she packed me and Louise into the car and took us to the hospital with her.

It was June, winter in New Zealand, and I could see my breath as we walked across the parking lot. Inside the hospital, though, everything was seasonless and stale. We followed Mum through corridors that went on forever, taking in glimpses of rolling metal carts, waiting rooms with people sitting in vinyl chairs. Finally, somewhere deep inside the hospital, Mum pushed open a swinging door, and we followed her into a room that smelled like disinfectant and was filled with beds, each separated by a curtain. From one curtain my grandparents appeared, but I barely registered them. My eyes were fixed on the hospital bed in front of me.

My tall, swaggering uncle now lay on his back, utterly still. His skin was pale. Only a few strands of hair peeked out from the bandages that wrapped fully around his head. His eyes seemed to be swollen shut. An accordion-like contraption rose and fell in rhythm with Uncle Mark's chest, and a plastic tube protruded from his neck. How could something that looked so uncomfortable, so *suffocating*, have been helping him to breathe? Behind him, machines beeped, recording vital signs I did not understand.

I stood still, trying to pretend that I wasn't frightened by the equipment and tubes. The grown-ups whispered among themselves, eventually stepping out into the hallway—maybe to talk to a doctor, maybe to talk to each other out of Mark's earshot, just in case. Louise and I were left alone with our uncle and all that machinery.

I studied Uncle Mark's face. I watched his eyes, his hands. I longed to see even the slightest movement; some sign that he knew we were there and he wasn't trapped. Once I saw it, I could tell the others. I could run out into the hall yelling, "He's still there, Mum! I saw his finger move! He must be waking up!" I knew exactly how everyone would react. They would all gasp, hugging each other with the relief of it all. They'd rush to my uncle's bedside, crying with joy. That's what they would do, if only I could just see him move.

But Uncle Mark did not move. Looking back, I think that's when I began to understand two truths: First, that wishing for something, even as hard as you can, isn't enough to change reality. Second, that a person's life can be altered forever, sometimes tragically, in the blink of an eye.

Weeks passed, but my uncle remained unconscious. Mum's answers to my questions grew sadder, less hopeful. With no signs of improvement, the doctors became increasingly convinced that Mark's brain was dead; without the machinery and equipment, his body would likely follow. My mother was at the hospital when my grandparents made the impossible decision to turn off their only son's life support.

That night, after Mum returned home, I listened to her describe to my father what had happened. She'd been watching through the small window into Mark's room as the medical professionals began shutting down the equipment. The accordion that had been allowing him to breathe stopped moving. Everyone expected his body would shut down too. Instead, my uncle began to cough, gasping for air. Seconds went by as Mum watched—seconds that she said felt like minutes, like an eternity. The coughing slowly subsided, replaced by a rasping. Then eventually, finally, a rhythm.

He was breathing. Uncle Mark was still alive.

Over the weeks that followed, the extent of my uncle's injuries became clearer. He eventually woke up, but he was now legally blind, and he'd suffered significant brain damage. But these were all words. The reality was different. I watched my uncle try to eat and drink again, I saw him struggle to click the top of a ballpoint pen while he laid in bed, and I looked on as he learned how to walk. He would never again live without support or care. And for now, that care would come from his family, including my mum.

Yes, everything could change in the blink of an eye and that made everything feel more fragile.

Around then, my stomach began to hurt. In my mind, it was as simple as that. I had a sore stomach. In the past, when my stomach hurt, the pain came and went. But now I felt it all the time. Morning, night, in between. Whenever I felt it, I would tell my mum. Sometimes she let me stay home from school, even though she and my dad were both working harder than ever.

Eventually, she took me to a doctor, who asked me questions and poked at my stomach while my mum hovered behind him, her brow creased. When the visit was over, Mum decided I would drop down to half days at school. *Good*, I thought. *Mum understands I don't feel well.* It would be years before my mother told me what the doctor actually said: that persistent stomachaches are a common way that children express stress.

I wasn't sick, it turned out. I was worried.

But while everything going on in Mum's family felt overwhelming, Dad's family remained a source of stability and routine. Just as in Murupara, Louise, Dad, Mum, and I spent three hours at the Mormon chapel each week. Now that we were closer to family, when services were finished, we headed over to see Nana Gwladys and Granddad Harry, my dad's parents.

My nana was a proud woman. She always said her own mother had come to New Zealand from Scotland with just three things: her son, a pistol, and her violin. I never heard much about my great-grandmother, but I imagined her exactly as my nana had been: fearless, funny, and a little bit frightening.

Nana had a deep gray perm that she had set every Friday in town; sometimes the chemicals turned her hair a slight tinge of purple. Her home, next to Te Aroha Domain, a large park, wasn't fancy, but it was dusted, polished, and always vacuumed to within an inch of its life.

Nana spent most of her time in the kitchen. Food was her love language, and sometimes she spoke it forcefully. If there were road workers on her street, Nana would bake scones and make tea, then head out to them, instructing, "Now, come and sit down for a minute, boys. Have something to eat. Come on now!"

In her own home, in a small alcove near the back door, she kept a stack of baking tins that I was sure were magic. They were filled with the most delicious, buttery shortbread, and no matter how much shortbread Dad and I ate, they never seemed to be empty.

Nana was almost never without an apron tied at her waist, woolen slippers on her feet, and her beloved orange-and-white fluffy yappy dog Dinky scurrying around. "Get out of it, Dinky!" she often snapped as she moved about the kitchen. Even those Nana loved most got yelled at from time to time.

But no one earned Nana's wrath more than what she described as "blue-tongue Tories." Nana joined the Labour Party in 1938 and had been the chair of the local party, holding meetings in her front room. She believed in looking after those who worked hard and had less, in a government that helped people in times of need. That meant supporting people when they didn't have a job, providing housing for people who couldn't afford rent, and making sure everyone could afford to go to the doctor when they needed, all progressive policies the Labour Party stood for. Nana wasn't shy about taking on those she didn't agree with. Apparently whenever Robert Muldoon, the conservative prime minister of New Zealand during my earliest years, appeared on the television, she'd stand up and snap it off before he'd even said a word.

Nana and Granddad Harry had seven kids. Of all my aunts and uncles, Marie took after my nana most. Marie was just as political, just as outspoken. She was a smoker, a straight talker, and always immaculately dressed. She wore high heels so often she claimed to be more comfortable in them than when her feet were flat on the floor. Even Marie's slippers had little kitten heels. She always wore long-sleeved blouses and pants that covered most of her legs. But sometimes when she bent over or scratched her arm, I could see deep scars.

I knew the story of the scars: When Marie was four years old, she'd found a box of matches in the shed where my nana washed clothes in an old copper tub. Somehow her tiny fingers managed to light a match, and her polyester dress caught on fire. Eighty percent of Marie's body was burned that day, and she'd spend the rest of her life in and out of surgeries. Maybe that's why Aunty Marie was so bold and brassy, often sprinkling her sentences with swear words that were new to my ears.

While there wasn't much cursing under my parents' roof, there were plenty of impassioned debates. No matter what was happening on the orchard, or with homework, Mum expected us all to be at the table for dinner at six p.m. sharp—*six o'clock on the dot!* Mum always yelled, impatient when we weren't there promptly to sit down for one of her steady rotation of meals: schnitzel; lasagna; tuna casserole; or corned beef in the Crock-Pot, served with mashed potatoes and chopped cabbage; and eventually, fried rice thanks to a night class she took in Chinese cooking at the local college. As dinner began, we'd turn on the news so Mum and Dad could listen to what was going on in the world.

Louise wasn't a fan of television, and she didn't care for the six o'clock news bulletin. "Isn't the whole point of a family dinner to spend family time together and talk?" Louise sometimes complained. "Not to sit around in silence with the TV on!"

"Shh," Mum would snap in response. "We're listening to the news!"

Sometimes it was Mum who couldn't stay silent, though. Mum wasn't overtly political and didn't have the same conservatism of her parents. But she held tightly to a worldview that valued fairness and common sense. Once in a while, she'd hear something on television that infuriated her, and all hell would break loose at the table. If there was a high-profile court case whose outcome she found inadequate, she might shout at the television, "Who judges the judges? *Who judges the judges?!?!*" Mum was usually a slow, methodical eater, but in these moments, she'd wave her fork in a frenzy. Once, she became so worked up that a corn kernel got stuck in her throat, which she needed medical assistance to dislodge—a fact my dad never failed to remind her about.

"Careful, Laurell," Dad would respond calmly. "You're going to end up back at the hospital."

"I'm just browned off," Mum would say, furiously shaking her head and returning her fork to the side of her plate. "Sometimes the people in charge just really brown me off."

For the most part, I watched quietly, trying to take it all in. I had never been overseas, never been on a plane, never even left the North Island of New Zealand. But from my kitchen table, I watched the reports of major events from around the globe. I didn't always fully understand these stories, but they still left their mark. The town I lived in, the life I had seemed so far away from what I saw on the news each night. And yet, it didn't. So long as there were people in the images, I felt somehow connected to them. They were also showing me something. *The world is so big and life could be fragile*, I understood. *But not so big that individuals couldn't do something to change it. Especially if we could find just the right way to be useful.*

4

What If It's Okay to Not Have All the Answers

WHEN I WAS eleven, my family showed up at Nana's house for Christmas lunch. As usual, Dad parked behind Granddad Harry's car, with its personalized T AROHA plate. I climbed out of the car, expecting to find Nana as we always did: in the kitchen, preparing the roast.

Nana whipped up delicious lamb with potatoes and buttery cabbage, rice puddings, fried scones with golden syrup. Somehow, she managed to cook all this on an ancient coal range. The range had flecked green enamel and cream doors, and Nana used it not only to prepare meals, but to heat all the water for the house. Granddad Harry always sat quietly nearby. Occasionally, he stood, picked up a poker, swiveled open the iron lid on top of the range, and fed it some coal from a copper bucket.

But today, although the air was filled with the usual fragrance of bubbling fat, Nana wasn't in the kitchen. Instead, she was seated in the lounge, in her favorite chair, an old olive-green rocker. A wool tartan blanket covered her lap. The room was quiet, and the grandfather clock in the hall chimed loudly. Nana's eyes were closed, and she rocked quietly back and forth in the chair. Her curls were more limp than usual, pressed down at the back of her head, a sign that she'd been sleeping. But it was her complexion I noticed the most. My nana had turned yellow.

I peeked into the kitchen. Pots and pans were spread across the counter, and the roast was in the oven. On the table were plates and cutlery. *Good*, I thought. *She is just resting. Everything is normal.* But even as I told myself that, I knew it wasn't true. I had heard Mum and Dad discussing her health that morning. They'd mentioned her liver, tests, and an illness I'd never heard of: *cirrhosis.*

All the grown-ups were chatting, carrying in bags of food and Christmas presents as if everything was okay. No one mentioned how Nana looked, her odd complexion, or how quiet she seemed. I watched Dad walk from the kitchen to the small alcove near the back door, to where the biscuit tins lived. He shook one of the tins, then pulled the top off and peered in. He picked up a small pale finger of shortbread, held it between his teeth, and put the tin back.

Nana mostly slept through that visit. When she woke, she smiled, gave the odd instruction, ate just a little, and insisted she was fine.

The next time we visited, Nana was seated outside on the stairs at the back of the house, taking in the sun. She wore her usual blouse, cardigan, and skirt. Slippers on her feet. *Good*, I thought. *She's better.* But when I approached her, I saw Nana's skin was even darker. Her legs swelled around her woolen slippers, and I could no longer see her ankles.

While I stood on the steps, Dad stopped again in the alcove, reaching up to the biscuit tin above the freezer. He gave it a little shake, but apparently this time, he heard nothing. He quietly placed the empty tin back on the shelf.

As Dad moved farther inside, I bent over and placed my arm around my nana's shoulder so I could give her a proper hug, the way I always did when greeting her. Instead of wrapping an arm around me, her head went limp and fell against the side of my leg. I stood there, as still as I could, so she could rest.

My nana is resting on me, I thought. My usually proud, strong Scottish nana was resting on me.

A few weeks later, I stood in a pew in the Anglican church in Te Aroha, listening to the sound of bagpipes fill the air. I recognized the hymn: "How Great Thou Art," a classic Scottish devotional, a fitting farewell for the most Scottish woman to have never visited Scotland.

She would have loved this, I thought. Maybe she did love it. Maybe she was watching us right then, shaking her head at all the sadness.

I believed in God. I believed in a heaven. I believed that was where Nana had gone. So shouldn't I have felt happy for her? She wasn't sick anymore, wasn't tired, and most importantly we would see her again. But even as those thoughts ran through my mind, the tears still came.

After the service, as everyone spilled out of the church and into the wide-open street, Louise and I stood outside, watching my dad and his siblings mill around the hearse. Aunty Marie's back was to me, but I could see her shoulders rising and falling unevenly. Dad's face was largely hidden behind aviator glasses, but as he helped roll the casket into the back of the hearse, I was pretty sure he was crying.

I noticed these things. But I didn't linger on them. I would spend the rest of the day distracting myself—spending time with my cousins, writing in my journal, and trying to find a locket Nana had once given me, with a plastic silhouette of a woman at the front, the sort of image that would have been found on a Victorian brooch. Although inexpensive, that locket suddenly seemed like an heirloom jewel. But all the while that same question nagged at me—a question that was simple to ask, but the implications of which felt too big to comprehend: *If I'm certain I'll see Nana again, if I really believe it, why do I feel so sad?*

Other parts of my life were changing fast too. As Louise became busier with school and new friends, our eighteen-month age gap seemed to widen, and she was less interested in playing with me. I began to spend more time with a feisty, bright-eyed, dark-haired girl named Fiona. She was confident, cool, and edgy; she listened to bands I'd never heard of and had great comic timing.

She had a twin sister named Penelope, as well as an older brother named Theo, who looked like a young Leonardo DiCaprio. Theo had been in Louise's class in school, and the shy way Louise talked about him told me she'd noticed his good looks too. When Theo started at boarding school, it only added to his mystique.

Middle school was the perfect place to share a classroom with Fiona. The two years between elementary and high school must be some of the best years of any child's education in New Zealand. You're not yet old enough for real exams, but you are mature enough that the adults let you loose with chisels in woodwork classes, knives in home economics, and needles in sewing. In middle school, we produced endless flans, paper clip trays, and pillowcases.

One afternoon Fiona and I sat down on the classroom floor as our teacher began the lesson by placing a cassette in a boom box. When she pressed play, we heard a simple, upbeat guitar, followed by a man's voice. *Now I've been happy lately, thinking about the good things to come.* The musician, our teacher explained, was named Cat Stevens.

Fiona loved music, and I wondered if she knew this song. My parents listened to bands from the 1960s like the Platters and the Carpenters, but this, *this* I had never heard before. I sat with my legs tucked underneath me, my blue tartan uniform hanging over my knees, listening as he sang about the edge of darkness and a peace train that was coming to take us all home again.

On one side of me, kids fidgeted and chatted among themselves. Not me. I leaned forward, listening to every word as he sung about *the world as it is.* Something about it felt oddly familiar—the strumming, the urgency in the melody, the chorus of voices. I closed my eyes, trying to drown out the noise of kids around me so I could hear every verse. Every word. *Why must we go on hating?* As the chorus built again, so did something in my chest. It expanded outward and upward, before it eventually hit the back of my throat.

Oh no. I was about to cry.

I looked around. Was this happening to anyone else? Was anyone watching me? My face felt hot, which I knew meant it was turning red. *No one should cry at a song,* I told myself. *It's just a song. Why would I cry over a song?*

The feeling wasn't entirely new. In fact it happened to me all the time. But until now, it had almost always happened at church. I had been taught that this overpowering feeling, this rush of emotion, was the Holy Spirit. But here I was, in my public-school classroom, listening to a song that didn't seem to have much to do with the Holy Spirit at all. As the song ended, I wiped at my cheeks, glanced at Fiona, and tried to pretend I hadn't just been crying.

To this day, emotions occasionally wash over me like a tidal wave, sometimes out of nowhere. I don't always understand them or know why they have arrived. And that was the case for "Peace Train." I have no recollection of why my teacher played that song that day. But the song—and my inexplicable tears—stayed in my mind for years after.

The world was changing fast. The Soviet Union had collapsed, and maps were being rewritten. A war in Bosnia started, and there was a deep famine in Somalia. Behind the harrowing images on the nightly news, I heard some of the explanations for them, but they never seemed to explain anything at all. Especially when the pictures were of children in the midst of wars or without food.

When World Vision, an international organization to fight child poverty, started a fundraiser that schoolchildren were encouraged to join, I signed up. I went to my neighbors, friends' parents, and relatives, filling an envelope with coins. This act felt so small though, so insignificant, and was always accompanied by a nagging persistent thought. *Someone should do something.*

In New Zealand, debates were raging over something called "The Mother of All Budgets." The government collects taxes from people to pay for all sorts of programs that the public relies on, everything from running the post office to building roads to paying for medicine to buying books for classrooms. Members of parliament debate and pass laws about how much money to collect in taxes, how to spend those tax dollars, and how much to provide to which programs; really, the government budget touches nearly every aspect of people's lives, and the positions you take on it say something about your values. The Mother of All Budgets was a set of proposals by the conservative government then in power to slash government funding. It would mean, for instance, that people who lost their jobs or who were too sick to work would all receive less support. And so would their children.

This was all on top of other changes—for the first time people were having to pay for hospital visits, and the cost of going to university was increasing. Students began protesting on university campuses. I saw passionate young people link arms, sometimes holding their ground even as police officers in helmets came crashing through.

I could connect so many of these headlines to the people I knew and even to my family: I had been in the hospital. It didn't seem fair that my parents might end up with a big bill because of me, for something they couldn't help. Or that my sister, the first one in my family who would go to university, might have to take a big loan just to afford it. But the only way I could articulate things in those days was that it just didn't feel *right*.

Then one day, I saw in Dad's discarded newspaper a political cartoon: An exaggerated image of a woman, whom I recognized from the news as Finance Minister Ruth Richardson, above a bubbling cauldron of soup. Before her stood a line of small, hungry-looking children, each holding a bowl. But instead of receiving soup *from* the cauldron, as one might expect, Richardson was making them pour what little they had back in. I was still too young to understand the details of what was being proposed, but my reaction to this cartoon was swift and instinctive. I knew New Zealand already had plenty of children living in poverty. I'd seen them in Murupara, and I saw them in Morrinsville too. Now the government was planning to end benefits these families counted on, programs that helped *children*. Again, it didn't seem right.

By the end of middle school, I was no longer merely watching the news, I was talking about it. My friends didn't especially want to talk about politics and world events, but sometimes their parents did.

Those days, I went over to Fiona's house all the time. The door was always unlocked, and it was assumed that when I arrived, I'd just walk on in. I did that hundreds of times, always with an awkward "Hello?" from the entranceway. Fiona's dad, Stephen, had an office right there, so sometimes he was the first to greet me. Stephen was a member of the conservative Association of Consumers and Taxpayers, so my opinions were often the polar opposite of his. As I grew older, our back-and-forth on what was in the news increased, but it always ended the same way: with Fiona finding us and calling time on the conversation.

Fiona took after her mum, Vicky. She had dark brown eyes, olive skin, and short, fashionable hair. I, by contrast, had a mouthful of braces to rein in extreme buckteeth, a tendency to turn tomato red anytime I was self-conscious, and the remains of a terrible self-inflicted spiral perm. Fiona was also a loyal and true friend, and not only did she sit by my side for hours while I was getting that terrible perm, but she also spent at least as many hours convincing me that it looked great, and no, it *absolutely* did not make me look like a mousy version of Orphan Annie.

On my way back to the room Fiona and Penelope shared, I always peeked into Theo's room. Though he was usually at boarding school, sometimes I spotted him hanging around in a tatty old bathrobe, a jar of Nutella in one hand and a spoon in the other, his shaggy blond hair hanging over his eyes. I liked Theo. He didn't say much, but when he did, it was typically to make a wry observation, or to poke a bit of gentle fun at Fiona. I tended to keep my mouth shut when Theo was around though, afraid to say something stupid. Apparently Louise felt the same. When she took her driving test, she'd run into him on the way out of the testing station, and she'd asked him how he did. "I failed," he told her, head down.

That night, Mum insisted Louise call him to cheer him up, maybe invite him to a movie, and Louise had recoiled at the idea. "I can't call Theo Lindsay! How embarrassing!"

I hoped to be as effortlessly cool as Theo when I was fifteen. But for now, it was enough trying to navigate braces, a bad perm, and—by 1994—high school.

Morrinsville College, the only high school in town, was just a few blocks from my middle school, but with six hundred or so students spread across five grades, it felt like a whole new world. Louise had already been there for two years. At fifteen she had long, wavy brunette hair, long legs that made her a graceful jazz ballet dancer, and the smarts that got her to the top of most of her classes. She also had a small streak of rebellion—at least I thought so. She rolled up the skirt of her uniform for starters. All of this made Louise exactly the right person to hammer with questions as we hurtled toward my first day: *Where do the first-year students sit? Can I say hello to you if I see you? What about Mum, can I just go to the canteen whenever I want?* For the last few years Mum had worked managing the school canteen—a cramped space tucked under the school hall packed with granola bars, potato chips, meat pies, and sausage rolls.

Each morning, as Mum arrived to find pallets of meat pies waiting, I made my way to the area outside the science block. There, I'd find my friends milling about, waiting for the bell to ring. In the warmer months, we'd sit on the benches that ran alongside the classrooms, and suck on Juicies—frozen plastic tubes of tropical fruit juice. By the time the June cold arrived, we were shivering, pulling up our long white slouch socks to keep our legs warm against the damp air.

On one of those cold June days, I showed up to find my classmates standing in a group, their voices low. It was clear that something big—something *serious*—had happened. I swung my green canvas bag under the bench as a tall, curly-haired girl named Sarah spotted me. She moved toward me. "Jacinda, have you heard?" Sarah's voice was urgent, and her cheeks were red.

Had I heard? It was so early. What could have possibly happened before nine a.m.?

"It's Fiona," Sarah said. I stiffened. I had no idea what would come next. "Her brother killed himself."

Surely, Sarah must have said more than this. In my memory of this moment, though, she vanished after the one sentence.

Theo, I thought. *Fiona's brother is Theo, who is clever and handsome and so funny. Who is quiet like my sister, who has model airplanes on his shelves and band stickers on his dresser, who eats Nutella straight from the jar and sometimes wears a cheeky smile. Theo.* The lightest fog hovered over the fields in the distance, damp and silent.

I picked up my bag and ran. I cut past my math classroom. Past the place I would line up for metalwork. Through the quad and down into the short alley that led to the canteen, and to my mother who was bagging up pies. *Mum will know what to do.* But of course, no one, not even my mother, could fix something like this.

A short time later, I stood on Fiona's doorstep, Mum's Toyota backing down the driveway.

Mum had called Fiona's house from the canteen. She'd spoken with Stephen, who'd confirmed that yes, it was true. I should come over, he said. Fiona wanted to see me. The door was open as usual, but I felt almost like an intruder, too close to the front line of someone else's grief.

I took a deep breath and I knocked on the door as I stepped inside. Upstairs, the living room was packed with adults. Even more adults stood around the black lacquered dining table, and yet more were in the kitchen. Their voices were murmurs, their faces a blur. From that blur, Stephen's face emerged. He gestured toward the back of the house. "The girls are in their room," he said simply.

As I passed Theo's room, it looked the same as it always did: the grid-line wallpaper, the green desk chair, the stickers, several of them half scratched off, as if Theo had changed his mind about them being there in the first place. The cheerful floral curtains that Vicky must have picked out for him, the schoolbooks sitting haphazard on the shelf.

Theo's room, with Theo's things. They were all so real.

I could hear the television on in the girls' room, some kind of daytime show. I pushed open the door and dropped my bag in the doorway. Fiona and Penelope spun around. Fiona's hair sat damp against her face, her eyes were red and swollen. I opened my mouth, but found I had no words. Until this moment everything about our friendship had been simple and easy. We'd played together, hiked, danced, and watched movies. We'd sung stupid songs, read fashion magazines, listened to the latest hits, tried to pretend we were grown-up. But for all of that, we were kids.

What do you say in a moment like this? Maybe you say nothing at all. Maybe it is enough simply to lock eyes on one another, then move toward one another and hug and fall to the floor. Maybe for a long while, that's all you do: cry. And when the tears slow, just for a moment, maybe you reach into your backpack and pull out three white crumpled bags of peach candies, which you'd taken from your mum's canteen promising to pay it back so you'd have something to offer, anything, even if it feels so small and stupid. Maybe then you each open a bag, still having said nothing, take the candies, and put them in your mouth, as if everything is normal, even as you all understand that nothing is normal, and nothing will ever feel normal again.

Maybe you just do that.

Fiona asked to spend that night at my house. Her home was too crowded, too overwhelming, too sad. As we lay quietly in the darkness of my bedroom, for the first time, Fiona asked about my religion. Where I believed people go when they die. I told her what I thought to be true: that there was a God, and there was an afterlife. A place where we get to see our families again. I told her this, because I believed it, and also because it seemed like the right thing to say. How else, I wondered, could anyone get through something like this?

But a few days later, I was at Fiona's house just before Theo's funeral, when a guest made a comment about God over lunch. Vicky had been in the process of serving soup and bread, and while I cannot recall what the guest said, I remember they were trying to offer comfort, the same way I'd tried to comfort Fiona.

At the mention of God, Vicky set her ladle down on the table. "God?" she asked. Her voice was sharp, strong, but it quivered as she continued. "If there is a God, how could he take my son? How could he . . ."

Instead of finishing, Vicky slammed her hand down on the dining table so hard the forks and knives jumped. In the silence that followed, no one looked at one another. My mind started reeling, searching for an answer to her question. *If there is a God, how could he?*

I had been a committed member of my church my entire life. I'd never once doubted the existence of God, or the truth of the religion that had been a part of my family since Nana first spoke with Mormon missionaries long before I was born. The only thing I'd ever doubted was the strength of my own faith.

I had always been taught that everything that happened was a part of God's plan. If there was a question you couldn't answer within your faith, then you just weren't meant to understand it. And that simple view had been enough. Until now.

I still believe in you, God, I remember thinking. *But I do not understand this. I will never understand this.*

Perhaps sometimes, there are no answers.

5

What If You Could Face Your Fears

WHEN I WAS ten, on one of our adventures together exploring the forest by our home, Louise and I found a discarded treasure: two cardboard boxes, about the size of the apple boxes Louise and I had struggled to carry. They lay on their side, contents strewn across the pine needles. Supermarket flyers. The boxes contained hundreds and hundreds of flyers, each advertising weekly sales at the nearby Four Square market. The sort of flyers that Four Square paid someone to place into mailboxes. But whoever was responsible for them apparently had chosen instead to dump the flyers here, on the floor of our forest playground.

I asked Louise what we should do with them. But my sister, for all her age and smarts, didn't seem to know either. "Should we show Mum?" she asked. We dragged the boxes the few hundred meters home, our arms straining. There, Mum picked up a flyer and frowned. On the outside of a box, she found a faded sticker with a phone number. She picked up the phone and began to dial.

"My name is Laurell Ardern. I live in Morrinsville, and my two daughters just found some of your leaflets in the woods . . . Yes, two boxes . . . Completely full, yes . . ."

The flyers, it turned out, belonged to a local delivery company. They'd noticed one of their routes hadn't been getting their leaflets but weren't sure why. Now they understood: The kid they'd hired to distribute them had discarded them immediately. And now, it seemed, we'd gotten him fired.

Before Mum hung up, she paused, the receiver pressed to her ear. "Yes, they'd be happy to do that. Yes, I'm sure."

She hung up the phone and turned to me and Louise, an awkward look on her face. "Well, girls. They asked if you would take over the delivery route. I said you would." Just like that, I had my first paying job.

Each week, I loaded up my bicycle and headed off with Louise. The bike wobbled from all the added weight of flyers as we headed to the two hundred houses that made up our route on the far side of town. The route took hours. And all of that would have been fine, except for 22 Lincoln Street. Or, to be precise, the *rottweiler* at 22 Lincoln Street.

It was one of my first days on the job, and I'd just grabbed a flyer from the pile and was ready to stuff it into the mailbox when I heard an unmistakable growl. I looked up, and there he was: the largest rottie that ever lived, moving toward me and snarling. He looked like the angry tire of a monster truck—all momentum and sharp teeth. "Louise!" I cried, pedaling like my life depended on it. "Louiiiiiiiiiise!"

Calling out to Louise was pointless. She hated dogs, so would hardly be coming to my rescue. Sure enough, when she eventually spun around from farther up the street, the look on her face said, *Jacinda, please sacrifice yourself to that beast so it doesn't get me.*

I dreaded Lincoln Street after that. Some days when I reached number 22, I sat across the road, trying to spot the dog before crossing. Other days I deployed a different tactic, waiting at the bottom of the street and then engaging my full strength to race past the gate, tossing the leaflet behind me as I went. I strategized, and sometimes I even prayed, but the animal always seemed to be *right there*—if not always in reality, he was unquestionably there in my mind, ready to take a chunk out of my leg.

Still, for all my fear, I never skipped number 22. I couldn't. Delivering a leaflet to that house, and every other house, was part of my job. To do otherwise would have been wrong. It felt like cheating. I would be letting someone down, somewhere, and if I did that . . . well, who knows exactly what might happen. I would certainly feel terrible guilt.

Looking back, I can see how silly that seems. Did the house at number 22 even *want* that supermarket flyer? For all I knew, the owners chucked it in the trash before they even reached their front door. But in my child's mind, that flyer represented the clear divide between right and wrong. Between doing what was expected of me, and not. No matter how much grief it caused me, I had to deliver it. That was the only way to stay on the proper side of the divide.

I would love to say that as I grew older, I learned to apply more balance into my relentless sense of responsibility. That I began, sometimes, to behave more like Louise had in the face of that rottweiler, able to say, "Thank you but I won't, in fact, head straight toward the terrifying jaws of my greatest nightmare."

But if I had, I suppose my story would have unfolded very differently.

In the meantime, feral rottweiler or not, *everyone* got their flyer.

If stuffing flyers in mailboxes seemed scary at times, that was a sure sign I hadn't thought about how terrifying it might be to go beyond someone's gate. That's because I had never been door-knocking.

Mormons go knocking door-to-door to share their religion. By the time I was thirteen years old or so, it was *my* turn to knock on doors on behalf of God. My feelings on this were mixed. On the one hand, I always felt like religion was personal, individual. The closest I remember coming to discussing it with anyone outside my family was that night at my house with Fiona. But there were good reasons to door-knock too.

Sharing our faith was an important part of being Mormon, and that's who I was, through and through. Even when there were questions my faith couldn't answer, ones like Vicky's, my response was not to lose my faith, but rather to lean into it. So one day, when the local "elders," young men who were on a mission from other countries, asked if I wanted to join them for an afternoon, I said yes.

The missionaries that served in Morrinsville were mostly Americans, and universally kind and decent. They wore a uniform of sorts: black suits, white button-down shirts, ties, and black lapel name badges. For our afternoon door-knocking, I donned the kind of outfit I would wear on a Sunday: an ankle-length skirt and top. Then the three of us headed off to a solidly middle-class street filled with simple, mid-century homes. The neighborhood was exactly the sort where I might encounter people I knew from the corner store, the netball courts, or—heaven forbid—school.

I was nervous. The whole scenario was so unpredictable.

When you walk up to a front door, you have no idea who's on the other side of it. Will it be a stranger? Someone you know? Will they be hostile or polite? And no matter who answers, or how they feel about the fact that you're standing there, you have to begin talking about the most personal thing you can possibly share: your belief in God.

As the missionaries approached each door, I hung back, watching and listening. Often no one answered. If someone did answer, the elders always began the same way: *Hello, Sir/Ma'am. We're from the Church of Jesus Christ of Latter-day Saints . . .* Often, that's where the conversation abruptly ended too, with doors shutting in our faces.

When the door didn't instantly close, I'd inch just a little bit closer. I'd listen and see if there was anything I might add. I rarely did, though I nodded along from time to time. But no matter how hard it felt, I pressed on, pushing through my strong urge to skip houses, even though every door felt like the equivalent of Lincoln Street with a rottweiler behind the gate.

Although I didn't see the missionaries get much past their introductions that afternoon, I noticed that they ended almost every conversation in the same way: *Is there anything we can do for you today?* And every time, as I stood somewhere between the driveway and the door, I observed something: That simple offer changed the demeanor of the person standing in front of them. If the resident had been holding the screen door open just barely enough to peer through, they might, at that question, open it a bit wider. Or, if they'd been looking down at the dog they held back, wedged between their legs, that question, asked with sincerity, might make them glance up, even for a moment.

Someday, I would walk up the path or down the driveway of thousands of homes to knock on thousands of doors to talk not about God, but about politics. I would learn that I was right to be nervous about door-knocking, though not for the reasons I'd expected. It wasn't just the unpredictability of the experience that made it fraught, it was the intimacy. But that's also what made it special.

A doorstep is an insight into the edges of someone else's life. Scattered tennis shoes and upside-down rainboots at the back door tell you who lives inside; toys and schoolbags at the entrance are a sign of what kind of day it's been.

While I might have struggled with starting conversations about God and sometimes even politics, I would learn that if I was there to ask someone about *their* lives, what they needed, what would make a difference to them—well, *that* I could do. That I *wanted* to do. I could talk to the mother whose home was so poorly ventilated that streaks of condensation ran down the inside of her windows, and whose children were sick, possibly from mold. I could sit down with the man who had just moved off the streets and into his first home and discuss how the joy of shelter also contained the pain of loneliness. In fact, I could do these things without reservation. On those future doorsteps, I'd not only ask, but I would share: ideas that had been turned into policies, policies that might fix a problem. And when I did that, there was no need to hang back in fear anymore.

Learning to door-knock as a teenager had other benefits, as well. It made all other cold-calling feel a little less intimidating—like the afternoon before my fourteenth birthday, when my mother took me downtown to find a job.

That day, I'd returned home from school to find Mum waiting for me, still wearing her canteen uniform, an apricot smock with a cream cardigan. In her warm but no-nonsense voice that made it clear she had made up her mind, she said, "Darling, it's time you got a job—a real one." Louise and I were no longer delivering flyers—the sheer volume of them had finally overwhelmed even my parents—which meant it was time for something new. Not working would have been incomprehensible to Mum, and with my birthday looming, she'd decided I was simply "old enough."

Louise had been working for a while at a produce store called the Vege Bin, an open-air shop on the main street. There Louise restocked the fruit and worked at the cash register, weighing bags of produce as wind and cool air rustled in from doors that opened straight out into the parking lot. I knew two things about Louise's job: that she earned $5 an hour, and that despite the polar fleece she wore, she was always freezing.

But that was life, at least according to my mum. There had never been a time in Mum's life when she wasn't working—if not for money, then at least to serve. She'd worked on her parents' farm, under the impatient eye of her dad. As a teenager, she'd worked weekends at a burger bar down the main street of Te Aroha. She'd always hoped to be an accountant someday—and she certainly had the mind for it—but she'd never had the chance or the support to go to university. No one in her family had.

Mum had instead taken a "good local job" doing payroll at a service station in Te Aroha, then working as a clerk in the post office. Once Louise and I were born, she'd arranged her working hours around our needs. She'd filled in for sick teachers at the high school in Murupara, cleaned the police station, cleaned the Mormon chapel, and ran the canteen at my high school. My mother's choices were never about what she wanted, but rather what others needed or expected. Now, it was my turn to make myself useful by getting my own job.

"Grab your school reports and certificates," Mum instructed me.

"Which ones?" I asked.

"All of them."

In my room, I pulled out an old blue folder with plastic pockets and began filling it with anything I could find: academic achievements, an award for a pie contest at a school fair, an award for my lamb at Calf Club Day. All completely irrelevant, but into the folder they went.

The Morrinsville commercial district is only a bit more than half a mile long. There are no malls, no restaurant chains. Employment options for kids my age were fairly limited: There was the Chinese takeout, fish-and-chip shop, burger bar, stationery shop, appliance store, or gift shop.

It was a Friday afternoon. Shops were getting ready to pack down for the day. Meanwhile, the takeout stores were gearing up for their busiest shifts of the week. As I walked across the street to start near the corner, my blue folder tucked under my arm, I felt my stomach drop. Was I really just going to walk into a shop and ask for a job? That seemed almost as scary as knocking on doors with the missionaries.

Mum and I stopped first at the Golden Kiwi, a family-run fish-and-chip shop and a Morrinsville institution. In all those years its decor had remained almost entirely unchanged: fresh fish in the window, wood-paneled walls, red marbled Formica counters, and large wall menus. In the back of the store, a pair of swinging wooden saloon doors divided the kitchen from the sit-down restaurant, with its painted cinder block walls, vinyl chairs, and red-checkered tablecloths. At the Golden Kiwi, $5 got you an entire meal, complete with fish, fries, and a salad. If you were feeling flashy, you might spring for the fresh snapper. Regardless of what you ordered, you'd always encounter at least one member of the Covich family, who had owned the restaurant for nearly three decades.

As I walked in, a bell on the door jingled, a sound I'd heard many a Thursday night when my family bought our four pieces of fish and two scoops of fries. Already, the shop was busy, the smell of fried food and the ding of the cash register filling the air. Carol Covich stood behind the counter in a blue uniform, scribbling an order. She was short in stature, with cropped hair, like she didn't have time for any sort of fuss, and she moved with the air of someone you didn't want to mess with. Carol's husband, Grant, was in the kitchen, his jet-black blunt bangs and thin mustache visible above the saloon doors. Despite the activity, neither Grant nor Carol looked remotely flustered. When it was my turn, Carol picked up a pen and a small note-pad. "And what'll you have?"

I took a deep breath and placed my folder on the counter. "Hi," I said.

Remember, smile, just start a conversation . . . with this incredibly busy woman.

I swallowed, then smiled brightly. "I was wondering if you needed any . . . help?"

Carol eyed me, as if assessing whether I might be worth her time.

"You're looking for a job?" Carol picked up my folder and began flicking through my collection of certificates. Her eyes narrowed with each turn of the page, perhaps unconvinced that being good with baby livestock was any sort of employment qualification.

"Have you had any jobs before?"

"I had a pamphlet run," I offered. "I also helped out on our orchard."

She considered this, then set my blue folder down on the counter and slid it back to me.

"Well," she said. "We happen to need someone on a Friday from five p.m. till close. You'd take orders over the phone and at the counter, and also help in the restaurant. After close, you'd help with the cleanup. The job pays $5 an hour. If you come next week, we can see how you go. Can you do that?"

I nodded.

"Hold on then." Carol headed to the back, then returned with a uniform that resembled hers. "Got 'em at a garage sale," she said, holding it out toward me. "They're old nurse's uniforms, but they do the trick. Make sure you wear covered shoes; there's hot oil back in the kitchen."

And that was it. I had my first *real* job, or at least a trial run for one.

My relief at having gotten the job was almost immediately replaced by a new concern: *What if I messed up?* The Golden Kiwi could get busy, very busy, especially on a Friday. I pictured Grant making his way through a long line of order tickets, the phone ringing, all those impatient guests in the dining room. *What if I lose my job at the first shift?*

Mum had worked at a similar shop when she was a teenager, and she still remembered the basics of what I would need to learn. When we got home, she disappeared into the kitchen, emerging with a newspaper and half a cabbage. "Here." She opened a newspaper at the middle and dropped the cabbage in front of me. "Practice wrapping this," she said.

When I looked at Mum blankly, she sat down on the floor, placed the cabbage in the center of the newspaper, and wrapped it as expertly as if it were a gift—but without any ribbon or tape. The maneuver required not only firm folding but also a careful high-speed flip to stop the cabbage falling out.

"There," Mum said, satisfied. She sat back, admiring her handiwork. "Of course, with hot fries you'll really need to hold them carefully as you flip; otherwise they'll spill out the front. Now you try."

I unwrapped the parcel and repositioned the cabbage in the middle—*a poor substitute for fries*, I thought. But even then it was harder than it looked. I didn't fold the paper tightly enough, and as I tried to flip it, the cabbage tumbled out the side and across the floor.

Mum gave me a reassuring smile. "Give it another try."

Wrap, unwrap, repeat. Wrap, unwrap, repeat. I practiced the move dozens of times that night, occasionally pausing just long enough to contemplate how ridiculous the scene was: It was the night before my fourteenth birthday and here I was, seated on the floor of our living room, repeatedly wrapping half a cabbage in newspaper. And yet, even the absurdity of the situation didn't stop me.

There were so many things that could go wrong on a shift: Messing up a phone order, giving a customer the wrong food, failing to wrap properly—fries and sausages bouncing to the floor. Carol shaking her head, before eventually taking me aside mid-shift to say, "I don't think this is going to work out." There was nothing I could do to prevent any of those scenarios except to practice, so that's what I did. Repeatedly, until I could do it with ease, and then still a few more times just for good measure. *Wrap, unwrap, repeat.*

This, too—imagining every worst-case scenario, then facing those fears and working obsessively to prevent each of them in turn—would be training for an entirely different kind of job later in life. Practice itself became a way to beat back my worries, one I would return to again and again in the years to come. Like knocking on doors, like handing a folder to an almost stranger and asking them to put their faith in me, I was already starting to prepare for a role I could never imagine holding.

But in that moment, I knew only one thing: Soon there would be fries to wrap. So, I best keep practicing. With a cabbage.

6

What If You Could Choose Your Own Path

BY THE TIME I approached my senior year in high school, either the politics of the time intensified, or I just became more aware of them. I am sure Mr. Fountain, my high school history teacher who taught me about impostor syndrome, played a role too. Until he came along, my favorite class was metalwork. I was the only girl in the class, a fact I mostly ignored while I stood for long periods of time, protective glasses on, leaning into the lathe while metal shavings fell from my projects—a plumb bob, or paperweights. If anyone thought I didn't belong in that class, I chose not to notice.

Mr. Fountain came to Morrinsville College straight out of teachers' training and was from New Zealand's capital city, Wellington, which was enough to make him "fancy" in our eyes. Yet there was nothing pretentious about Mr. Fountain. He was only in his twenties, but he had already lost nearly all his hair. He wore small round glasses and strode into the classroom each day with the energy of someone who had drunk one more cup of coffee than they should have. Each period for him was a chance to bring a new lesson to life. Like the time he rearranged the classroom so it looked like the floor of parliament. Or the time he taught us about the history of India by printing off two opposing articles on the man who led India's struggle for independence from Britain, Mahatma Gandhi—one critical of the leader and the other a celebration of his accomplishments—and urged us: "Find out who he was. Find out for *yourself*." He wanted us to learn how to make up our own minds. Perhaps he also wanted us to know something else: that both people and history are complicated.

In those days, the history curriculum gave teachers some choice about what was covered in their classes. Rather than choosing English and European history, which was standard in most schools, Mr. Fountain often chose topics from New Zealand's past.

And so, in high school, I started to develop an understanding of the complex history of New Zealand. I learned about the signing of He Whakaputanga—a Māori Declaration of Independence—in 1835, as Māori sought to assert their sovereignty. I learned about the subsequent signing of the Treaty of Waitangi between Māori chiefs and the British Crown in 1840, a founding legal document of New Zealand that lives on today through interpretation by judges and lawmakers. I learned that the Māori-language translation of the Treaty, the version signed by almost all the chiefs, emphasized tino rangatiratanga, or self-determination, which was different from the English-language version. I learned about the nineteenth-century wars that followed the Treaty, including the British Army's invasion of the Waikato district where I lived, and the raft of discriminatory laws imposed by the settler government, which confiscated millions of acres of Māori land and alienated generations of Māori from their language and culture.

In all of this, Mr. Fountain highlighted the strength and innovation of Māori resistance to colonization: the development of new military tactics, the establishing of new political entities to build unity, such as the Māori King Movement, and the use of nonviolent resistance to oppose aggression and injustice. This history was dark, painful, and unresolved. It was also connected to stories that were in the news of the day. In other words, history wasn't stuck in the past or some chapter that had been closed; history was playing out still, all around us.

In 1995, when I was fifteen, there was a government apology to Waikato Māori for breaches of the Treaty of Waitangi, which included payment for the land that the government had taken. It was the first settlement reached between Māori and the government, and it triggered plenty of debate in the news. Reporters shoved microphones under people's faces in the street and asked if they thought settlement agreements were a good idea. Often you'd hear comments like *Isn't that all in the past?* or *We just need to move on.* There was a strange nervousness in these answers, as if addressing a wrong somehow made us, in the present day, guilty of acts from one hundred and fifty years earlier, or perhaps less patriotic toward our home. But learning New Zealand's history didn't change how I felt about my home country. In fact, it was in Mr. Fountain's class, lesson by lesson, that I realized loving where you are from meant seeing all the mistakes that had been made, all the wrongs that needed to be fixed, and all the ways that it could be better.

The more I observed, the more I started to share what I thought. And as I did, the more disagreements I ended up in—including at my own dining table. That was why my mum encouraged me to join speech competitions, including the one I almost missed because I got stuck in the bathroom stall. But despite my desperately dry mouth, my unending panic in preparation for competitions, and my impostor syndrome, I wound up getting the attention of the debate team.

I was fifteen at the time, in my third year at high school,

when the debate team's "first speaker" was unable to go to a tournament, so the team asked me to fill in for her. I'd watched the team several times and found it much more exciting than the monologues of speech competitions. Debate involved fiery exchanges between speakers, and quick-witted rebuttals, and even allowed interjections in which team members leaped to their feet and yelled, "Point of information!" Sitting in the audience, I often found myself forming arguments in my head, as if I was already onstage.

That first tournament was a regional one, which meant we'd be competing with teams from schools from all over the Waikato district. My teammates Anthea and Matthew were two years older than I was. Matthew barely needed to prepare the speeches he gave with a slightly posh accent even though he was the son of a truck driver. Anthea was thoughtful and meticulous, able to pick an argument apart piece by piece until there was nothing left. As for me, my job was to set the team up: lay out our core argument and then come back at the end to make a closing statement in what was called the "leader's reply."

There were very few things that didn't set my impostor syndrome into overdrive. But right from the start, I felt like debating was something I could do. The times I'd gone back and forth with my parents, and even with my friends' parents, about various issues meant I knew how to form and deliver an argument. My insistence on overpreparing meant I was going to be as ready as any person could possibly be. But it was more than those things. My brain's tendency to imagine every possible worst-case scenario—the very trait that in the past had left me obsessing about a snarling rottweiler or visualizing angry customers and spilled fries—meant I could envision not only a clear line of argument but also what might come back to me from the opposing side. Until now, my near-constant worry had felt debilitating. Suddenly, it felt like a superpower, something that could clear a path for me rather than hold me back.

We won that first debate, and when the regular first speaker got a scholarship and moved away, I became a permanent member of the team. I would not only debate for the rest of my high school career, I would also join the Waikato regional team for national competitions. Through the years, I'd debate on behalf of things I believed in and also on behalf of things I didn't. I'd debate issues of the day, issues that were purely theoretical, and issues that made me think: *That smoking should be banned. That New Zealand should withdraw from the British Commonwealth.* And one that I would come to think about often in the future: *That the difference between what we are and what we could be is the greatest waste.*

Debate would take me to places I never imagined. It would take me on a plane for only the second time in my life.

It would allow me to see the South Island of New Zealand and also the capital, Wellington. Through debate, I visited the New Zealand parliament and went to formal events and dinners that featured food like "pepper-encrusted Brie"—whatever that was.

Did my mouth still sometimes dry up so completely that I couldn't sound out vowels? It did. Was I often nervous? Always. Did my stomach hurt before every tournament, so much that I was often unable to eat that morning? Yes. But while this was the first time I'd found something that had turned what felt like debilitating weaknesses into a strength, it wasn't the last.

I was sixteen years old and had been at the Golden Kiwi every Friday night for more than two years. There was always a steady routine to these shifts. I arrived at five o'clock in my pale blue uniform: a smock, really, which hung just over my knees and had a zipper that ran the full length of the dress, from hem to the modest V-neck. Although Carol had claimed it was a nurse's uniform in a past life, I suspected it had been used in something a little closer to a nursing home cafeteria.

Grant cooked the fish, fries, sausages, and anything else that got plunged into the deep fryer. Another cook worked the hot grill, flipping burgers and steaks. Carol and I took orders by phone and at the counter, wrapped food, and scurried around to provide table service to seated customers. After the doors closed at eight p.m. sharp, we spent the next hour scrubbing tables and counters, sanitizing the window where fresh fish had sat on ice, counting the earnings in the cash register, and deep cleaning the vats, mats, and floors. After that, I usually went home and collapsed.

One Friday night, during my junior year of high school, I wasn't planning on going home as usual. I was headed to a party instead: the "head boy and head girl party." The head boy and girl were two of the most important kids in the school—elected to their positions by peers and approved by teachers and the faculty. Though the head boy and girl were official roles, like class co-presidents, tonight's party was a wholly unofficial event—a tradition that involved music, friends, and no chaperones.

I'd spent the shift watching the clock: Thirty minutes to closing. Fifteen minutes. Five minutes. I was finishing up in the kitchen when I heard the bell above the front of the shop jingle. I glanced over the saloon doors into the front of the shop, where a guy about my age was standing at the counter. Ordinarily, I'd be annoyed at someone entering at closing time. But I couldn't be mad at *this* guy. He was lean, with dark hair and a strong jaw. Plaid shirt, jeans. Green eyes fixed squarely on the menu, and I was standing in front of him in what was basically a smock. "Can I help you?" I asked, picking up an order pad and pen.

Hot Guy studied the menu. I studied him. He had a restless energy and swapped his weight from one foot to the other. His eyes darted nervously, even as he placed his order. Then, I tried my best to walk to the kitchen acting nonchalant. As I hung his order ticket with the others above the vat, I heard Carol in the storeroom organizing boxes. And then, behind me, I heard something else: the ding of the cash register.

Wait. There's no one else down there. Why would it ding . . . I darted back to the doors in time to see Hot Guy leaning over the counter, pulling cash out of the register with both hands. "He's robbing the register!" I shouted. Carol was at least a foot shorter and probably thirty years older than I was, but she moved like lightning. She shot past me and was right on his tail as he yanked open the front door and dashed outside.

"Give me back my money!" Carol ran after him. I followed too. Outside he climbed into an old brown Triumph that was idling on the far side of the road. And then he was gone, around the corner too fast for us to catch his license plate, leaving me and Carol in the middle of the empty street staring at the place where the car had vanished.

By the time the police came and went, it was late. I drove home, changed out of my uniform, doused myself with Impulse body spray to cover the smell of fried food, and headed to the party with considerably less enthusiasm than I'd had before the robbery.

The party was at the house of a student on the outskirts of town. Old cars lined up on the grassy curb, and heavy metal music blasted from a set of speakers. Behind the house, it was crowded, with kids in baggy jeans and printed T-shirts sitting in plastic chairs or leaning on hay bales. Many of them had been partying for hours, and the yard was filled with laughter and loud stories. Across the yard, I spotted my friend Ginny. "You won't believe what happened tonight," I said.

Ginny and I had become close years ago, doing a science project that measured whether the sun faded denim faster than washing it. Ginny was more a part of the popular crowd than I was. She had strawberry-blond hair and was intelligent, athletic, and studious. We sat down together, and I told her the story as we watched kids moving in groups through the dark. I recognized most, though not quite all, the revelers.

At one point, the head boy passed by, followed by a cluster of guys. In that entourage, I saw someone who didn't go to our school. He had dark hair, wore jeans and a plaid shirt, and had a nervous energy.

"Ginny!" I grabbed my friend's arm. "That's him! Right there!" It *was* him, the guy who'd just robbed the Golden Kiwi.

I watched as Hot Guy walked into the light of the veranda. He hadn't noticed me. I considered my options. I could go home and call the police. That was the responsible thing to do, and it was probably the fastest way for Carol and Grant to get their money back. But this was the head boy and head girl party, the biggest event of the year. The arrival of the police would end it all, and I didn't want to be the one responsible for that.

But I also wasn't going to do nothing.

"Hey, Gin," I said. "Could you pretend you're interested in him and get his phone number?" Within minutes we made up a persona for her, and she moved toward the veranda. I stayed behind, watching from the darkness as she sat down near him and began to talk. Soon, she was seated on his knee, laughing with her head thrown back. She was so convincing that I began to wonder if she'd forgotten why she was there. Then I saw her produce a pen. A few minutes later, she was back at my side, handing me his phone number. I raced out the back gate to my car.

Dad was in the kitchen when I got home. When I told him what happened, he spoke in a disapproving tone.

"Jacinda, you should have called the police." Still, he picked up the phone, dialed the number, and asked for the boy by name. The person on the other end—it sounded like someone's mum—apologized. He wasn't home at the moment; he was in Morrinsville, at his cousin's party.

Hot Guy ended up going through a youth justice process. He paid back the money he stole at a rate of $5 a week, and he apologized to Carol and Grant for the theft.

Still, that didn't stop me wondering about that night for months after. What made him do something like that? Did he even think about it, like *really* think about it before it happened? It wasn't the crime of the century, but still, why? These were questions that I'd seen my dad confront. Now they nagged at me too.

As I approached the end of high school, there was a choice to make: *What was I going to do with my life?* Whatever choice I made now, I was sure it would set the path I was on *forever*.

Over the years I'd considered multiple careers: attorney, youth aid officer in the police force, counselor. These were useful jobs. They helped people, and perhaps more importantly, they felt within reach. But was I ready to choose just one? So when it came to university, I considered getting a bachelor of arts, a good general degree that would allow me to study subjects I loved like history and politics. But when I shared this plan with my parents, Dad quipped, "Well, you better learn to ask, 'Do you want fries with that?' because that's the only job you'll get with an arts degree."

Dad wasn't being cruel. I knew that, even as I rolled my eyes at him. He just wanted me to have job security, the kind that he'd had in his decades-long career. My sister and I would be the first in our family to attend university. It felt like higher education had become an expensive privilege. If I were to take out a loan for fees or living expenses, the interest would begin accumulating immediately—before I'd even graduated—at a rate of around 7 percent. I wasn't sure I'd *ever* earn enough to pay off loans like that. I wanted a good job, a steady job, but there was a reasonable chance I wouldn't be in *any* job long enough to be well paid. After all, I thought, I'd eventually get married and have kids, and who knows what would happen to my career after that.

My sister was already engaged to her boyfriend, Warren, whom she'd met through the church. I liked Warren. He was shy and quiet and very sweet to Louise. I was happy for her, even if I was quietly sad it meant my near-constant companion and closest confidante was moving out. But her engagement reinforced what I had always been sure of: that success meant having a family. The only other thing that I felt sure of for myself was that I loved politics. By now, I'd watched two elections, and I knew I was firmly on the side of the Labour Party, the same party my nana had always supported.

I also had three jobs: my Golden Kiwi shift, a weeknight position cleaning shelves at a gift shop, and checkout cashier at a local grocery store. Sometimes our local Labour candidate came into my checkout line at the grocery store. He didn't have a shot at winning—not in a conservative place like Morrinsville—but I still eagerly talked politics with him every time I rang up his milk, cereal, and bags of apples.

But being *interested* in politics and *working* in it were completely unrelated things. Politics was the kind of thing, I was sure, you would do if you could afford to have a hobby. It was a passion, not a profession.

One day, after months of thinking about my future and getting no easy answers, I went over to nearby University of Waikato. I collected brochures from every degree program there. I read every one and began to narrow down my options. The management school was probably the best in the country. But that's not what I wanted to study. So I compromised.

On a bright spring day a few months before the year ended, I walked into Mum's canteen. She was sitting in front of a ledger book tallying the week's earnings, a small desk calculator with a roll of white paper printing out numbers nearby.

"Mum," I announced. "I've made a decision." I told her that University of Waikato was starting a new degree, a bachelor of communications. It would be hosted out of the management school but would allow me to also take classes in international relations.

Even as I said this, I still had no idea what I wanted to do. I figured my most likely path would be management communications, working as part of a comms team in some company. Was I excited about this? Not really. But I'd heard there were jobs in that area, and wasn't that good enough? It was so much more opportunity than my mum had ever had.

My whole life, I'd watched Mum put everyone's needs before her own. Mum had worked in the canteen for more than seven years. And after all those years, she earned a lower hourly rate than I did as a cashier at the grocery store. But only once could I remember her implying that she might have wanted something else. We'd been discussing her long-ago dreams of becoming an accountant. *It would have been so satisfying*, she'd said, *to prove to myself that I could.*

Now, Mum nodded along happily, ever my supporter. "Great," I said. I felt relieved that I'd finally made a decision. "That's what I'll do then."

I mean, what else would I do? Study politics? And then what?

And perhaps that would have been it for me and politics. But then I got a phone call that opened up a world of possibilities I had never imagined.

PART TWO

7

What If You Could Take the First Step

"LOUI-JACINDAAAA, can you get the phone?" Mum has done this for as long as I remember: mashed up my name with Louise's, always with the elongated vowel at the end. My sister got the inverse: "Jaci-Louiiiiiise." And not even Louise's moving out had restored me to plain old Jacinda.

"Got it!" I set down my linguistics textbook, which, truth be told, was painfully dull. I was in my first semester at university by now, living at home to keep costs low.

In the kitchen, I lifted the chunky white portable phone from its cradle. "Hello, Jacinda speaking."

"Jacinda Ardern?" The voice on the other end, a man's, was confident and chipper, like someone handing out prizes from a radio station. There was something vaguely familiar about it too, though I could not place it.

"This is Harry Duynhoven," said the voice.

Harry Duynhoven was a member of parliament, the MP for New Plymouth, down where Aunty Marie lived. She'd volunteered for his campaigns and was always proud of his strong majority, especially in a district that could be pretty conservative. In fact, before Harry's election in 1993, New Plymouth had voted Labour in only five of the prior twenty elections. Harry had earned the district's trust while crusading on practical matters that angered him, like secondhand car dealers who cheated buyers by winding back the miles on imported cars to pretend they were newer than they were.

And now Harry was calling *me*? Why?

"Hi, Harry! Lovely to hear from you." I winced. I sounded like someone expecting a package delivery.

"Your aunty Marie tells me you're interested in politics," Harry said, with the hint of a chuckle. I knew exactly what that meant: Marie must have talked about me like a proud parent. I could just hear her. *My Jacinda, she's a clever one, Harry. You should meet her.*

Yes, I told Harry, I was interested in politics, very, though the Labour Party in Morrinsville was pretty small so interest didn't translate to much.

"So you know that it'll be a big election campaign this year," Harry said. "An important one."

At that moment, the government was led by Jenny Shipley, New Zealand's first female prime minister and leader of the National Party. In New Zealand, there is only one lawmaking body—the parliament—and you need at least half of the seats in parliament to form a government. The leader of the biggest party then becomes prime minister. The conservative National Party had been the government for nearly a decade now. But after the election in 1996, they needed the support of New Zealand First, a smaller party led by Winston Peters, to form a majority. But that alliance had fractured recently, and people seemed to be tiring of the cuts that had been made to public services.

Now, in 1999, it seemed as if Labour might finally have a shot at winning. If they did, the Labour leader, Helen Clark, who had decades of experience and was as smart as she was serious, would become the new prime minister.

"I'm wondering if you'd like to come down to New Plymouth for a bit," Harry continued, "to help with the campaign."

I sat bolt upright. Just five short minutes ago, I was trying desperately to keep my attention on linguistics, wondering whether it was too early to go to bed. Now I was talking to an MP—an MP who, amazingly, seemed to think I could be useful.

Harry began explaining some of the tasks he needed help with. *Volunteer recruitment . . . phone calls . . . maybe some door-knocking when the campaign really gets going.* "And of course on election day we need help with getting out the vote; driving people to the polls, that sort of thing," he continued.

My mind raced. In my eighteen years, I'd learned to do a lot of things—prune trees, wrap fish and chips, ring up groceries—none of which would likely come in handy on a campaign. Also, I wasn't *from* New Plymouth. Mine was a dairy town. New Plymouth was mostly an energy hub, a place where thousands of people are involved with oil, gas, and mining. I knew nothing about those issues.

Then again, I also knew how to knock on strangers' doors and start talking to them. I knew how to work hard and not stop. And if I could help Harry, that meant I'd also be helping Helen Clark, the leader of the Labour Party, to win government. It meant giving Labour a chance to make changes to all the things I'd seen that *didn't feel right.* That meant an increase in the minimum wage, improving workers' rights, the chance to keep students from facing growing student debt. It meant *doing something.*

In the end, I voiced the only objection I could fully articulate. "My aunty is away," I said. Marie had taken a job in Australia, and I didn't know when she would return. In the meantime, I didn't know anyone else in New Plymouth, a three-hour drive away, and I didn't have the money to pay for accommodation.

"We'll find you a place," Harry assured me. He said this so simply, it almost seemed easy.

"Sure, Harry," I said. My stomach flipped a little as I said the next three words: "I'll do it."

In New Zealand, the campaign to elect a government and prime minister is short and intense. We don't have set election days. Each election must be held within three years of the previous one, but the date is otherwise chosen by the prime minister, who picks a Saturday based on everything from school holidays to rugby games. About four to seven weeks before election day, parliament adjourns and MPs head out to the campaign trail.

When Harry's campaign manager called me a few days later, he wanted me there as soon as I could arrive—well before the start of the campaign. They needed someone to recruit volunteers so they could hit the ground running once the campaign officially started. This volunteer recruitment could be done during my university break. Then, I would return to New Plymouth when the campaign officially started and stay for as long as I could. I swapped out my shifts at the supermarket, loaded up my Mum's Toyota Corona, and hit the road for the three-hour drive.

New Plymouth wasn't large, with fewer than seventy thousand people back then. But I'd grown up in a town that didn't have a traffic light, so it felt huge. I wound through the outskirts of the city, past the gas stations, hotels, and supermarkets, until

I reached wide suburban streets full of neat brick houses with white aluminum sunporches and gardens filled with jasmine and daphne.

This was where I would stay for the next few weeks, at the home of a volunteer named Lorna. Although I had never met Lorna until I knocked on her door, she greeted me enthusiastically, with eyes that smiled behind large wire-framed glasses. Lorna was probably my aunty's age, somewhere in her fifties. And she made me feel the way family might—waving me into the house, showing me a comfortable room with a tightly made bed.

For the next few weeks, I worked both at Lorna's house and the Labour Party headquarters, a small timber building with the feel of an old community hall. To the right sat Phoebe, Harry's electorate agent, who helped with casework. If a person in Harry's district had a problem with or question about some government issue—trouble getting their unemployment benefit, for example, or immigration issues—they might seek out help from their local MP. In Harry's office, Phoebe was there to help.

On the other side was Harry's office, not that there was much to the space. The room was sparse, without much natural light or a computer. I had the feeling that Harry liked to spend his time among people more than he did in this little room.

Down the hallway was a large open space with wooden floors, high windows, and a small, elevated stage on one side and a kitchen on the other. Although the kitchen was empty, I could imagine tea and cake being served from that bench, trestle tables scattered around the room, people milling about with red clipboards in hand and bright red Labour rosettes—a decoration that candidates and their representatives use to identify their party—pinned to their cardigans.

As I was standing there, it all felt strangely familiar, as if somehow I already knew that one day, years from now, I'd stand in dozens of rooms just like this one.

Campaigns need volunteers. A *lot* of volunteers. They're needed for leaflet delivery, door-knocking, phone-banking, and helping get out the vote on election day. Without volunteers, campaigns flail or never get off the ground at all. The Labour Party has thousands of members; the challenge is to turn these members into volunteers come election time. And it was my job to motivate supporters to give their time and energy to getting Harry elected. My tools were a large white portable landline phone, dozens of pages of an Excel spreadsheet with hundreds of names and phone numbers, and the ceaseless encouragement of Lorna.

On day one, I set myself up at Lorna's dining room table

with its white crocheted tablecloth while she moved around in the small kitchen nearby. I laid a blank piece of paper along the bottom of the first row in the spreadsheet so I could line up the name with the phone number, took a deep breath, and started to dial.

"Hi, my name is Jacinda Ardern, and I'm calling on behalf of Harry Duynhoven . . ." I began.

When the person politely said "no, thank you," and hung up the phone, I looked up to see if Lorna had noticed my call was cut short. She was still putting away breakfast dishes. I annotated my sheet with *no*, took another deep breath, tried to exhale my embarrassment, and moved on to the next name.

Good morning, I'm calling from Harry Duynhoven's office, to see if you'd like to . . .

Hello, would you be interested in doing a bit of leafleting for the Labour Party . . .

Hi, my name is Jacinda, and I'm volunteering for Harry Duynhoven . . .

One call after another. With each, I listened to how people answered and tried to start a conversation. *How do you think things will go at the election? What do you think might swing things?*

By the end of the first day, I had a script down. Not that every call was straightforward. The lists were three years old.

Sometimes circumstances had changed dramatically, and I discovered I had an uncanny knack for making those changed circumstances as awkward as possible. I asked someone if they could deliver leaflets, only to find they could no longer walk. When someone told me they couldn't leave their house, I suggested they be part of our phone bank where "we'd provide the call sheets," not realizing they were also severely vision impaired. Several times, I asked to speak to someone who'd died since the last election. I took careful notes, hoping to prevent any future caller from bumbling through as I did.

I kept going. I double-checked names. I dialed, marking down interests and availability in tiny writing at the edge of the spreadsheet. I smiled till my cheeks hurt, hoping my enthusiasm would be felt through the phone line. When I was met with sharpness or even hostility, I politely hung up, then muttered *No need to be so rude about it* to myself while writing *DNC* in large letters on the side of my sheet—short for *Do Not Contact.*

I spent hours at Lorna's table. Sometimes at the end of the day, I went to the Labour Party office where I typed in the responses from my spreadsheets. In my first week, I also attended a campaign meeting, where I met Harry for the first time. Harry was shorter than I expected, but as sprightly as he seemed on television. He moved constantly, with the boundless energy of someone who relished having too much to do. He was also joyful, smiling beneath his white beard, thanking everyone for everything—for the tea, for the biscuits, for one volunteer's "bloody brilliant work" on getting billboards up—and for my phoning.

Sitting in that first meeting, talking about the plan for the next few months, I felt part of a team—the critical back-of-house that allowed all the big, public stuff to happen. I felt *useful.* This gave me all the motivation I needed to keep going with the tedious job of making calls.

Near the end of week one, I was starting to feel like an old hand. I dialed a number, as I had done hundreds of times by now, ready to recite the script I now knew by heart. As the phone rang, I double-checked the name on the sheet in front of me.

"Hi, John, this is Jacinda Ardern. I'm calling from Harry Duynhoven's campaign. As you know, it's an election year, and we're gearing up for the campaign. I'm wondering, John, whether you'd be available to help?"

"Sorry, Jacinda," John replied. "I'm pretty busy myself."

They always said that. But by now, I'd roped more than a few busy people into one job or another.

"Of course." I kept my tone warm and friendly as I pressed on. "But we have even small roles that don't require too much time. They'd make a real difference!" I stared ahead, pen poised ready to jot down a job for John.

"Really," he insisted. "I am *quite* busy."

What could be more important than getting a new government elected? I thought to myself. *It's one day in three years!* "How about a bit of leaflet delivery in your own time?" I pressed.

"No, I . . ."

"Even working on the election day itself would make a huge difference. You know this election will decide whether we have another three years of a National government—"

"Look, I can't, Jacinda," he finally said, using my name for extra emphasis. "I am the Labour candidate for Taranaki-King Country."

I glanced at the name again. John Young. I knew that name. *Oh God, I've been badgering someone who's running for parliament in the seat next to Harry's.* "Of course you are!" I said, cringing. I tried to make myself sound natural. "*John!* I am so sorry, you obviously have your own campaign to run."

"Yes. Yes, I do," he said. He sounded deflated. I had not only pestered the man; I had made him doubt his name recognition. "Good luck with yours," he told me.

A familiar monologue of doubt started playing in my head: *That mistake shows I have no business being here.* My head was down on the table when Lorna walked in. "You okay?" she asked. I told Lorna about the John Young phone call. To my surprise, she threw her head back and laughed—a full-body laugh, the kind I might have expected from my irreverent Aunty Marie.

I kept going through those stacks of paper, my fingers double-checking one name after the next. *Peter . . . Graham . . . Susan. Election day, phone-banking, leaflets. Disconnected number . . . too sick . . . DNC . . .* The stack got smaller, and the list of campaign volunteers longer.

One day, near the end of my volunteer recruitment phase, I was inputting names from my most recent calls into a spreadsheet at the Labour Party office when I heard the door open. I peered out from around the doorframe to check if someone was there when I heard Phoebe's gentle voice. "Hello! How can I help you?"

An older man stood in the doorway. He wore a faded parka over worn slacks. His shoes looked like they were at least a decade old, and his face was covered in white stubble. He shuffled wearily into Phoebe's office, and I heard him tell Phoebe his story. He was a grandfather. His grandson lived with him. The boy attended school but struggled with severe asthma. He himself wasn't well enough to work, and he was struggling—with the cost of caring for a grandchild, with the cost of their home, and with illness too. He suspected the house was making them both unwell.

There were a few things Phoebe might be able do. For example, she could connect him with support for people raising children that weren't their own. If he was in a private rental, she could try to get him into state housing. But I also knew that government support wouldn't be enough, and that eight years ago, the conservative government changed the rules so people living in state housing were charged market rental rates instead of the lower rates charged by the government in the past.

In other words, for all Phoebe's work and good intentions, to *really* improve this man's life, the system itself would need to change. And that meant the government had to change.

That afternoon, when I finished my sheets for the day, I packed up and waved goodbye to Phoebe. I'd been in New Plymouth for almost two weeks now. But seeing this man, hearing his story, had driven home the stakes of this election, of any election. An election wasn't just something that was battled out on a television screen through slogans and attack ads. It wasn't just about phone calls or pages of an Excel spreadsheet. It was about real things that happened to real people. If Harry won—if Labour won—actual people's lives might be better.

I climbed into the car and dumped my papers on the passenger's side. As I started up the Corona, I had another thought. *What would it be like?* To not just help people one-on-one—by being a good community member and volunteer, as I'd seen my mum do her whole life—but to also have a vote and a voice in the place that set and changed the rules.

What would it be like, I wondered, *to be an MP?*

The thought disappeared as quickly as it entered my head. *Remember, you need a job,* I reminded myself. *Not a hobby.* I turned on the ignition and pulled away from the office.

A few weeks out from the election, I returned to New Plymouth. By now, Marie was back from Australia, renting a house on a tree-lined street with small brick-and-timber homes. The neighborhood bordered the local technical college, and Marie's rental was across the street from the campus radio station. On hot days when the windows were open, I could see the broadcasting equipment, as well as students in headphones talking into large microphones.

When Marie first arrived in New Plymouth more than twenty years earlier, she was a recently divorced single mum with two kids. There had been a housing shortage at the time, and for three months, she and her kids had lived in a camper van while she searched for a place to live. Every day, she'd drop the kids off at school, then head to the housing corporation office with the hope that they could help. Eventually, they moved her into state housing in Marfell, one of New Plymouth's poorest areas.

Living in Marfell had been a huge eye-opener for Marie. There were occasional shootings and stabbings. Windows were smashed regularly. There, Aunty Marie planted a huge vegetable garden where she grew everything from chard to pumpkins. Whatever she grew, she shared with her neighbors. Before long, she was a fixture—the lady whose garden bounty was open to anyone. When she joined the local Labour Party in the early 1980s, it was Marfell where she always wanted to door-knock.

In every district, there are places that seem easy to campaign. Flat suburban streets where almost everyone has already enrolled and has a voting plan. But those were the places my aunty Marie put at the bottom of her list.

"You go where people need the most help," she told me as we headed to Marfell to knock on doors for the first time together. She marched confidently onto streets where nearly everyone lived in publicly funded state housing, to get them enrolled and ready to vote.

Marie had been working on Labour campaigns for years. Her first campaign was alongside my nana in the 1970s, when Helen Clark was running for a parliament seat from Piako. One day, years back, while door-knocking in Marfell, Marie came across a woman whose home had a hole in almost every wall, no heat, a broken toilet, a broken shower, and a damaged stove. Marie returned, then she kept visiting, building up a relationship with the woman. Eventually, Marie helped the woman access support and fix her home; the holes were repaired, the shower and toilet repaired, the kitchen redone, carpets all pulled up, floors all varnished. New curtains and drapes. Painted inside and out.

When last Marie visited her, the woman's son—a senior member of one of the motorcycle gangs—was visiting. He'd been in prison while the home was being fixed. Instead of leaving them to their visit, Marie didn't miss a beat. She talked to him about the election too.

Day after day, Marie and I walked the streets together, knocking on one door after another. It was Aunty Marie who taught me to shake gates when arriving at a new house. *Just give it a little rattle*, she explained on our first day. *If there's a dog, it'll come out, and you'll be able to tell if it wants a piece of you.* And so I would shake, confidently, with purpose, trusting that all my rattling would protect me, even from a creature as mean as the Lincoln Street rottweiler.

It was all as exhilarating as it was exhausting. Meanwhile, all the people I'd been calling to get involved were coming together and doing the work of the campaign: leaflet delivery, phone-banking, door-knocking on weeknights and weekends.

One night we were sitting in the campaign chair's front room, chairs pulled up around a coffee table, running through an agenda of items. "How are our stocks of signage looking?" he asked.

"Good," said the person who kept an eye on the campaign placards featuring Harry's smiling face. "Only a few needed replacing this week." It was a bad look if the candidate's image had been defaced, so a team of people phoned in any vandalism to the signs.

"Right then," the chair continued. "We have some local advertising underway. Papers and the like. Any other thoughts on those?"

Generally, I had stuck to the things I was asked to help with: keeping the lists of volunteers, knocking on doors, helping Marie organize election day get-out-the-vote efforts. But I had been thinking about this.

"Well, I was thinking that student radio might be worth considering," I offered. Labour had proposed removing interest from student loans while they were still in school to make university more affordable. I went on: "It's just that the student loan policy will impact every polytechnic student who has a loan. I'm not sure many students even know about it. Perhaps we could run an ad on the polytech's radio station."

Harry nodded. "Good idea. Do you think you could write something?"

"I could have a go."

"Why don't you voice it too? Better coming from someone young than from someone crusty like me!"

It didn't take long to get the ad up and running. Sometimes

I heard it while driving around town. Then one afternoon I was driving back to Marie's when I didn't just *hear* the ad, I also heard the announcers talking about it. They were still discussing it when I arrived back at Marie's, so I got out of the car, walked across the street to the station, and approached the open window of the booth. I could see two young men, headsets on, microphones sitting in front of them. I stuck my head in the window. Only briefly second-guessing myself, I greeted them.

"Hi! My name's Jacinda," I said. "I'm the one who voiced that ad." The announcers moved a microphone closer to me, and suddenly I was having a live discussion on the radio, with my head still poking through the window. I hadn't been in politics very long—a few weeks in total as a volunteer—but I was already in a groove. I'd taken one step, saying yes to Harry, which led to the next—making calls and occasionally messing them up—and then another and yet another, and now I was chatting on the radio about policies that mattered in real people's lives, policies that *felt right*. I don't recall what I said exactly, but I remember how much I loved that moment: being able to explain an issue that I felt strongly about, and about which I thought every young person should feel strongly.

I paid attention to everything, every detail. I pored over newspapers. I reviewed policy announcements, aware that I might be asked about issues when knocking on doors. I attended community meetings and memorized local facts and figures. I didn't want to just be a *volunteer*—I wanted to be a source for any information an undecided voter might need.

I also began to appreciate how much personal connection matters to people. In New Plymouth, people knew Harry. When people learned I was there on Harry's behalf, they often had a story to share. Harry had visited their workplace or their school. He'd helped get them into a new home. Once, I visited a house and found the owner kneeling in the front garden. When she found out why I was there, she stood up from her weeding and came over to tell me that when her husband had died a few years back, Harry had sent her a card. She'd kept it on her mantel for months. She didn't know how Harry knew about her loss, but it mattered to her that he did.

As we moved from house to house, Marie and I, like all volunteers, kept meticulous track of which voters said they'd likely vote for Labour in the booth. Come election day, we knew we'd want to check in with these supporters, make sure they actually got to the polls. If they hadn't, we'd move heaven and earth to get them there. In a country as small as ours, seats could be won or lost by five votes—or even just one.

By the final week of the campaign, I could see even my aunty growing weary. She'd sit for just a moment in the morning, a mug of instant coffee in her hand. Then a few minutes later we would be out the door. The countdown continued. *This is my last Saturday before election day*, I thought to myself. *This is my last Monday, the last candidate's meeting, my last leaflet drop, my last time bundling a door-knocking pack.* With every hour that ticked closer to election day, the excitement and the tension ramped up.

I love election day. I love everything about the act of voting. I love seeing the culmination of so many people's hard work. I love seeing the people who come to work for the Electoral Commission this one time every three years, who take the role of helping people vote so seriously. I love seeing the election monitors sitting there with their rosettes on from all the different parties, volunteering their time just to make sure that everything's running smoothly.

I love knowing that people of all ages, from all over New Zealand, and from all walks of life, will be doing one thing, all within a few hours of one another. I love seeing the little orange VOTE HERE signs everywhere on the corner of streets and next to schools, community centers, and town halls. I love seeing people stream toward these polling stations, the excitement of checking in with other party volunteers, all across the country, asking each other: *How's it looking? How's the turnout? Is it a sunny day? Yeah, let's hope the rain holds, because if it rains, it's a disaster.*

And then, you step into the little cardboard booth, pick up that bright orange pen, and make a check mark. I always have an emotional response to that. Always. Behind that check is so much toil, so much at stake, but also so much hope. I love everything about election days, and for me, it all started in New Plymouth. Not only my first campaign, but also my first vote.

On election day, Aunty Marie and I rose early. The nearest polling station for us was just around the corner at a boys' school, but we took the car. Marie knew we had a day of running around ahead of us. After we walked inside, I took my ballot from a trestle table and walked to the cardboard booth, picked up my large orange pen, and voted for Labour.

After, we walked outside as gray clouds rolled in. Marie's head was down and her eyes were glassy. "Your nana would have loved this," she said, almost to herself. She dabbed her eyes, then shoved her handkerchief back in her bag and fished out her car keys.

"Right then, girl," she said. "We've got work to do." We got into the car and headed to Marfell. We had voters to mobilize.

Later that night, Aunty Marie and I sat together at the

Labour headquarters—the same place where I'd made thousands of calls. Red balloons hung around the hall. Tables were dotted around the edge of the room with small shallow wineglasses, plates of sausage rolls, and bowls of potato chips. Marie kept her eyes firmly on the projector screen as the results were coming in. She was silent, focused.

Then New Plymouth's numbers came across the screen, and Marie let out a "yeeeesssss!!" Harry smiled at the back of the room while everyone else burst into spontaneous applause. Harry had kept his seat.

In a few hours the news got even better. Labour had defeated the National Party. That meant Helen Clark, the Labour leader, would take over as prime minister from Jenny Shipley.

I look back on this now, and I think how absolutely remarkable this was: In my short lifetime, I'd been able to see not just one woman reach the highest office in the nation, but two. Because of them, it never occurred to me that my gender would stop me from being involved in politics. Or that it wasn't possible to be a woman and to lead.

My personality—all my weaknesses—on the other hand, well, that was a whole other story. And that was why for now, my campaign work was done. It was time to focus on my studies and on getting a job.

8

What If You Could Follow Your Passion

BEFORE MY FINAL year of university, I visited the study abroad office and picked an exchange program that would allow me to finish my degree by spending a semester in the United States at Arizona State University. The American academic calendar didn't quite match New Zealand's, which meant I'd have several weeks to fill before heading to the States. My friend Alex, who was fearless, untroubled by what-ifs and self-doubt, suggested how I use that time. "Why don't you go to Wellington for the break?"

"And do what?"

"Volunteer. Contact Harry, tell him you want to help in his office." Alex made it seem like calling an MP and inviting myself to work in parliament, six and a half hours from home, was simple.

But maybe it *was* simple. Louise and her husband, Warren, were living in Wellington now, so I could stay with them.

And what was the worst thing that could happen? As if she were reading my mind, Alex pressed, "Just ask. What do you have to lose?"

"Okay," I said. "I will."

A few weeks later, in early 2001, I arrived in Wellington—a city full of suits, cafés, bohemian creativity, and wind—for my internship in parliament. There, government work is done across a four-building complex near the waterfront. The most iconic of these government buildings is the Beehive, a 1970s building that looks exactly as its name implies, cylindrical and tapered.

Harry's office, though, was in the adjoining and more traditional Parliament House, a beautiful century-old neoclassical building with a massive staircase marking the entrance. I'd been in this building for a debating tournament in high school. There, I'd taken photographs with my parents on the stairs and peeked briefly into the parliamentary debating chambers. I'd been a tourist then, a mere spectator. Now, as I stepped into the building, it was different. I had a role to play, a *job*.

I walked inside and took a long moment to look around. It felt so grand: marble walls and pillars, bold tile floors, arches and busts. Everything was bustling, a little echoey, *important*-feeling. I felt like I'd just walked behind the curtain of a play I'd been watching my whole life.

Harry's office was on the third floor, far from the hurried energy of the lobby. I paused at the door; a formal panel spelled out his name in gold lettering. I wondered how special it must feel to have your name on a door like that, the letters *MP* sitting boldly at the end.

I can clearly remember those quiet moments before stepping into Harry's office, but my memories of the rest of day are a blur. Harry's secretary, Mari, gave me a tour through the maze of buildings and hallways, talking briskly as we went: *Down there is the mail room, here's the select committee corridor, this is the Grand Hall where MPs host events. That's the Legislative Council Chamber, library's over there, Bowen House is that way, and of course ministers are in the Beehive.*

Mari also rattled off all the rules I needed to know. *No using the elevators when the bells ring for question time at two p.m., it's MPs only. No stepping into the "ayes or nos" lobby! Also we need to make sure Harry has the order paper for question time.* I nodded as Mari spoke, asking no questions whatsoever.

It became clear that while I knew the fundamentals of our parliamentary system as an outsider, there was a whole raft of things that the insiders knew. The rules of the debating chamber. Where to walk and where not to. How to address people. *Better not to ask anything,* I thought, *than reveal the depth of my own ignorance.* If I wasn't going to ask, I decided I'd have to get my knowledge a different way: by reading a guide called *Parliamentary Practice in New Zealand*, a book that was nearly six hundred pages long. I took it home on that first night and began to study it intensively.

But all my studying and quiet attempts to absorb the peculiarities of the parliament's traditions didn't protect me from occasionally screwing up. Once, I walked down the speaker's hallway when the bells were ringing to call all the MPs to the chamber for question time. Those chimes meant the corridor was to be clear, but I didn't fully understand that. Suddenly the speaker of the parliament appeared in the hallway along with the parliamentary clerks. One of them caught my eye and mouthed "run," so I scuttled back down the hall while the bells tolled and people in cloaks swept past me. I was both out of breath and embarrassed, and I desperately hoped no one else saw me racing down the hall.

During that internship, I helped a bit with Harry's correspondence, opening and logging mail, sometimes typing out replies. I ran errands and retrieved papers from Harry's mailbox, and I even helped with his electorate newsletter, which included issue updates for his constituents.

At Mari's suggestion, I began to join daily morning teas with the EAs (executive assistants) in Copperfield's, the café in the Beehive, where they all drank tea and ate cheese scones as big as my hand. That's where I heard that Phil Goff's receptionist would be out of the office for a few weeks. Did I want to fill in for her? Phil was an MP from Mount Roskill, a skilled politician, and a devout member of the Labour Party. I'd always admired Phil. As a young man, he'd sported long hair and a thick mustache, riding his motorbike to protests and marches for social justice causes. Today, he was one of the senior ministers in the party.

That's when my internship moved from Harry's quiet, regal nook to Phil's bustling concrete office in the heart of the Beehive where I took over the phones.

Phil was the minister of justice and of foreign affairs, so the calls that came in ranged from how to appeal a conviction, to complaints about the sentence handed down for a high-profile case, to human rights issues in Tibet. I did my best with these calls, diligently finding the answers—or at least finding the person who could.

But I discovered that MPs often got an entirely different kind of call, one for which there was no good response. These were the calls from people who were convinced of some dark truth that was being hidden from the public. These callers were often distressed and sometimes angry. I remember picking up the phone one day to the voice of a woman who was clearly upset. She believed that the government held a record of her having taken a supermarket cart, or at least I think that was what she was telling me. She believed she was on some kind of list, that she was being watched, and could I take her off *that list* please?

I asked other people in the office how we could help this woman who called so frequently. They knew her, and they knew other people like her, they had tried, and no, there was nothing we could do. You can't, after all, remove someone from a list that doesn't exist.

At the time, I didn't stop to wonder what would happen if there was ever a platform big enough to unite individually distressed callers. A place where everyone who believed in a list could come together and reinforce their beliefs with one another. Or, God forbid, if someone came along and manipulated those people, played on their distress for their own gain. I just thought of the one person on the other end of the phone that I couldn't help and felt incredibly sad.

My internship passed quickly. But by the time Phil's receptionist returned, I had begun to learn the rules of the debating chamber, I knew where the select committee rooms were, and I had eaten far too many scones. Each night, I returned to my sister's home feeling exhausted, my mind spinning with things I'd learned and people I had met. But in spite of all the confusing rules and my fear of making a mistake, I loved it. It was a place where laws changed and problems were fixed. And not just on paper, but for people—like the ones I had met door-knocking in New Plymouth. Yes, politics had a hand in the poverty I had seen all those years ago in Murupara, but I felt sure that politics could also fix it.

As I packed my bags for my semester at Arizona State, I felt lucky to have seen politics up close, lucky to have seen the inside of the *machine*. But that also made it a chapter that was harder to close. *An internship does not a career make*, I reminded myself as I stuffed clothes into a suitcase. There were so few jobs in politics, and even then, what made me think I could do any of them?

When I graduated university after my semester in Arizona and returned to New Zealand, Phil Goff offered me a job. I would be a researcher and help with things like writing his newsletter. It was entry level, but an exciting chance to work in politics. Though I still couldn't quite believe I belonged there, I hung on tight to this opportunity. I rented a room in a home in Brooklyn, a neighborhood on the sloping outskirts of Wellington, with two old friends, as well as two complete strangers. It had a collapsing veranda and hot tub full of green algae. But none of that mattered especially, because it didn't take long for my whole life to become about politics.

I worked all the time. This was easy to do, since Phil kept such long hours. By seven thirty a.m. he was at his desk, poring over the *Herald* and *The Dominion*—clipping articles out of the newspapers, underlining sections he wanted to discuss with staff, scribbling little notes for us in the margins. As a minister, he had a nine-person staff, and his office was always humming. Everyone bustled around, chattering into headsets. But even after most of the staff had left, Phil stuck around, wrapping up his day sometime after ten p.m., at which point he'd head out for a quick game of squash "to clear his head." On weekends and holidays, Phil was famous for baling hay and repairing fences around his property outside of Auckland. He was the definition of an "active relaxer."

Phil never asked any of us to work long hours. But I wanted to. The only breaks I took from the office were outings with people my age from other MP offices. We'd sit in the Beehive bar, simply named 3.2, having a rapid-fire back-and-forth about new legislation and political gossip.

I was still what you'd call a relatively junior advisor in those days. I was in my early twenties, and as much as the political work thrilled me, there were some days I was reminded how unsuited I was for it all. This feeling had started when I was just an intern and returned as soon as I began working full-time at the Beehive. Early on, Phil's advisor, a longtime political operator famous for his cleverness and cynicism, had asked me to distribute a report the Ministry of Justice had created on the impact of a recent change to a law about underage drinking of alcohol. "Start with government MPs," he instructed; Labour was in power, so that meant the MPs who were on our team. "When that's done you can get them out to the opposition too." I studiously worked through the afternoon, labeling and stuffing envelopes. I did just as he asked: getting the report first to Labour, and only then to the opposition National Party. By the end of the day, I had distributed the report to everyone. When Phil's advisor heard this, he was furious. "The report was embargoed," he steamed, arms in the air in a state of anger and disbelief. "You weren't meant to give it to the opposition *today*."

As the advisor stormed into Phil's office to rant about the "disaster" his new staffer had caused, I walked quietly to the bathroom stalls, closed the metal door behind me, slid the lock into place, and burst into tears.

It wasn't just that I was new. Being in politics for any amount of time, at any level, required toughness. That was true whether a person was on the front lines, like the MPs, or like me—back of the house, behind the scenes—little more than a cog in the machine. Pitfalls lay everywhere. Your political opponents were constantly waiting for any missteps that could be exploited and amplified. Critics were relentless, and public sentiment felt like it could shift so quickly and so easily. I was sure a person needed a spine of steel to survive in these halls, and so long as I was crying in a bathroom, I was sure I didn't have that.

And yet in what other place was there a chance to do as much good for as many people? I still thought all the time about that moment in New Plymouth, back when I was eighteen years old, listening to the stubble-faced grandfather describe to Phoebe all his difficulties as he cared for his grandchild. It was the first time I had seen politics for what it could be—a way to change things both for one person *and* for hundreds of thousands of people. And to do that for all the issues that mattered to me—like poverty and inequality—in what other job could that ever be true?

So I did my best to mask my doubts and sensitivity. No one would ever see me cry in a bathroom. To the outside world, I apparently came across as someone with promise—a hard-working member of the Labour Party, bound to move up, possibly becoming an MP herself one day. I began to hear comments. *She's a hard worker, that Jacinda.* Or: *She's one to watch.* Or:

Could be her name on the door one of these days. But in these moments, I often looked at MPs like Phil, and I saw the long hours he put in, the constant meetings and events, the unrelenting criticism from people who thought he was doing too little and also those who thought he was doing too much.

One day, driving to Auckland Airport after a difficult public meeting, I watched from the back seat as Phil laid his head against the headrest, exhaling heavily. He turned around, looked at me wearily, and rubbed his forehead. "Jacinda," he said, "if they ever ask you to run, don't do it."

"Ha," I said. "You don't have to worry about *that*, Phil."

About a year later, I left Phil's office and went back to the office of Harry Duynhoven, but this time I took a job as political advisor, a promotion. By now, Harry was a member of the prime minister's cabinet; he was the associate minister of energy, as well as the associate minister of transport, so my day-to-day became more about issues of energy safety and extraction of oil, gas, and minerals. I learned about permitting mines, offshore drilling, and laws about government management of minerals. I went to energy conferences, visited oil rigs, suited up in hard hats and coveralls, and sank hundreds of feet into the earth, where the air felt damp and heavy. This work had its own challenges:

I didn't always agree with the policies I had to work on, I was almost always the only woman anywhere I went, and I felt like I constantly had to prove myself. But I kept my head down and just kept going.

In 2004, I became active in a campaign supporting a civil union law, which would allow people of the same sex to marry. It was through this work that I got to know Grant. Grant Robertson was Prime Minister Helen Clark's political advisor. He was one of the most important people in government, but you'd never know it by the way he acted. He was never too busy to stop and talk, to ask how you were. Looking out for people like an informal mentor was his specialty. The only tell that there were a thousand other things Grant needed to be doing was the way his eyes, every so often, might dart around a room.

Grant was always slightly disheveled, with a frequently untucked shirt and an occasional coffee stain. He had a broad, friendly face and thin-framed glasses, and he was known for his deep love of sports and music. He also happened to be openly gay.

Grant had grown up closeted in the South Island city of Dunedin and had been at various points bullied, isolated, and depressed.

It was as a young person that he'd watched as parliament passed the Homosexual Law Reform Act in 1986, which had overturned laws that made being gay illegal. The political fight to pass that law had been ugly, charged with almost unspeakable cruelty from MPs like Norman Jones, who once in a speech said looking at gay people was like "looking into Hades . . . Don't look too long—you might catch AIDS."

I often wondered what it must have been like for a young Grant to sit in front of a television hearing those words. And yet whenever he talked about this period in history, he talked about how *validating* it was. As if the cruelty of the debate was outweighed by the outcome and by the fact there were MPs willing to fight for LGBTQ+ rights. Perhaps that was just one of the reasons he was now working so hard to see a civil unions law pass. But as I watched him at work, I had no idea he was keeping half an eye on me, clocking the passion I had for my work.

9

What If You Could Be Sensitive

I HAD BEEN working for the government for two years, first for Phil and now for Harry, when Grant called me and asked to meet at the Beehive café. It was a Friday, so parliament wasn't in session. With no MPs around, Copperfield's didn't have the usual bustle. People lingered a little longer at their tables, decompressing from the busy week. When Grant showed up, he was in his "casual uniform": jeans, canvas shoes, and a dark wool sweater.

Grant ordered a black coffee—knowing him now as I do, I realize it was likely his third for the day. I didn't know why we were meeting, exactly, but when Grant asked me how things in Harry's office were going, I told him the truth. I was looking for a different job. Harry was a good man, but I found myself pushing back against him a bit too much and a bit too often; it wasn't just that he opposed the civil unions bill—that was, after all, for him to decide. It was that he wanted to work on policies that weren't part of the government's agenda.

Grant listened attentively, nodding along as I talked. His eyes were tired but warm, filled with empathy, as if he were saying, *Hey, I've already got the world's problems on my shoulders, so feel free to share yours with me too.* In the years that followed, I would see this side of Grant repeatedly—not just with me, but with everyone around him.

"I don't know what I'll do next," I said. This was true. I didn't have a clear career plan, not then and not ever. "But I've applied for a job in the youth development ministry." It wasn't my dream job, but I liked working on policy.

"Well," Grant said. He nodded like he already knew I'd been job hunting, and I suppose he probably did. "I was thinking we could use you up on the ninth floor." The ninth floor of the Beehive was a rarefied place. It's where the prime minister sat, where decisions got made, where few people visited and even fewer worked. Now Grant Robertson was offering *me* a job there. The position was a junior advisor; I'd do research, help with the planning of Helen's days out on the road, and support Grant.

It was 2005, an election year, and it had been almost six

years since Labour had taken the reins of government. Under Helen Clark's leadership, the party had achieved a lot: a tax credit for families so they would have more income, increases in the minimum wage, a national retirement fund, and the beginning of an agreement with China to boost New Zealand's industries through increased trade. But this year Helen would be running against a new opposition leader, Don Brash, who'd made a late entry into politics after running the Reserve Bank of New Zealand.

To say I wasn't a fan of Brash was an understatement. He felt so outdated and detached from the lives of New Zealanders. He attacked the welfare system and the people who needed it. He had said he would abandon New Zealand's long-cherished position against nuclear weapons, and worst of all, he'd famously made a speech to the Ōrewa Rotary Club about Māori issues, which struck me as pure race-baiting. Brash had no business being prime minister. But he had made big gains in the polls.

Now, in Copperfield's, Grant finished the last of his coffee, lifted his eyebrows over his glasses, and asked, "So, would you like the job?"

I was terrified. I understood the pressure of political work and how tough you needed to be, and that would be even more pronounced up on the ninth floor. But there was no better place to be during an election than right in the thick of things, and I desperately wanted to help Labour stay in government and keep Don Brash out.

I said yes immediately.

Helen Clark was known for her long hours. Rumor had it that she slept only four hours a night. She'd dedicated her entire life to public service. She was smart, strategic, utterly unflappable, and a phenomenally hard worker.

Perhaps that was why when I first moved up to the ninth floor, I rarely saw Helen. I worked just a few steps from her office, but I never went in there.

For the most part I got my assignments instead from Helen's chief of staff, Heather Simpson. Outside the Beehive, few people knew of Heather, and she liked it that way. But inside these halls, she was infamous and intimidating, known for her directness, intellect, and biting humor. She was so influential that people called Helen and Heather H1 and H2, and the joke was that no one could agree on which of them was which.

Heather had a no-frills approach in just about every respect. She wore neutral colors, no makeup, and wire-rimmed glasses over which she peered when assigning a task. Early on, Heather called me into the office to assist her. I don't even remember what it was about, just that I took furious notes, trying desperately to get down every bit of information, and deliberately nodding to prove just how well I was getting everything Heather was saying. At one point, Heather paused. When I looked up, she was staring at me, unblinking. "Do you understand what I have just asked you," she began, "or will you leave this office and spend the next thirty minutes trying to figure it out?"

I swallowed. "The second one."

Heather sighed, exasperated, and began explaining the task again but with a faint smile. I could tell she at least appreciated my honesty.

I was a week into the job before I finally sat face-to-face with the prime minister. I had just attended a controversial hearing with the chief executive of the education qualifications authority (NZQA). The previous year's scholarship exams had an inexplicably high failure rate. This had caused an uproar among students and parents, and now politicians were being asked what they knew about the problem. Helen was preparing for question time, the hour in the debating chamber where she would be questioned by the opposition, and there was a chance she might be asked about the hearing, so I was brought in to give a summary. I followed Grant and Heather into the prime minister's office, where Helen sat at her boardroom table. In front of her was a cup of tea and an egg salad sandwich, the same lunch she ate every day, as well as an array of documents.

This is it, I thought, taking a seat. *A chance to meet Helen properly. I'll tell her that my nana worked on her first campaign in the Piako seat. That Nana was chair of the electorate committee and once had a photo with a Labour prime minister too, and it was on the front page of the* Piako Post *and oh how happy and proud she looked. And she's gone now, passed away in 1992, but I know she'll remember her anyway—my nana—Gwladys Ardern. And I am Jacinda Ardern, and I'm so thrilled to be here.*

But I had forgotten. Helen was the woman who, once, when the doors of a Defence Force plane she was traveling on flung open in midair, simply gathered her papers so they didn't fly out the door. Helen was focused, and in one hour, she would be grilled by the opposition. There was no time for reminiscing or sentimentality. She looked at me, held her pen above her page, and said just one word: "Go."

At the end of the briefing, Grant and Heather filed out. I was packing up my papers to follow them when Helen stopped me. "How do you say the name again?" By now it was just the two of us in the room. *This is my moment,* I thought, stopping by the door, *my chance to introduce myself properly.* "Jaaaaaaciiiiindaaaa Arrrderrrrrn." I said my name slowly, sounding out each syllable methodically. Helen held my gaze for a moment. She gave a quick head shake, a slight look of both confusion and disbelief on her face. "No," she said matter-offactly. "How do you pronounce Van Rooyen? The chief executive of NZQA?"

By the time I had walked the thirty feet between Helen's office and the office I shared with Grant, my face had turned beet red. I didn't even need to tell Grant something had happened; he could see it. When I told him about my uninvited attempt to introduce myself, he let out a spluttered laugh and slapped his leg. "Ohhh," he said between snorts, "that is so good." His reaction made me smile too, and it calmed the furious thumping in my chest a touch. Somehow, I knew then that Grant was going to help me get through whatever errors in judgment and protocol lay ahead, and there would be plenty. When you find your people, you don't let go.

The stakes felt enormous on the ninth floor. A wrongly typed digit or misplaced word in a budget, a clumsy phrasing of some policy detail, all had the potential to land Helen on the front page with some terrible headline. *That* could give Don Brash a narrative he could exploit. In this new role, I often scheduled events for Helen, and I feared bad photo ops as intensely as I'd once feared a snarling rottweiler. This wasn't an imagined problem. I remember watching Don Brash on the news one night. He had visited a raceway, donning a pair of overalls for the event.

But to get into the racing vehicle, he had to climb over the cage. I cringed, almost feeling sorry for him as I watched him struggle to climb in, eventually lifting his own leg over the frame so he could get into the car seat.

Even Helen, shrewd as she was, wasn't immune. I remember watching the six p.m. news one night and questioning whether we should have sent her into a chicken factory when hairnets were involved. Thankfully we had a distraction; Harry was standing next to Helen in a completely ridiculous-looking beard net.

Once the 2005 campaign got started, all of these high stakes took on new urgency. The polls were neck and neck. I spent most of my time by Grant's side, hunched over my computer until my shoulders and wrists hurt. Night after night, I stayed up until the wee hours of the morning with Grant and Heather, writing campaign briefs and policy releases, stuffing briefing packs for campaign announcements.

One of the policies we had been working so hard on would remove interest on student loans entirely, a step further than what had been done in 1999. To promote the policy, Helen visited university campuses, events that could sometimes be chaotic. One day, she visited the University of Canterbury in Christchurch. I sat in the office with Grant, watching the event on the twelve p.m. news.

The office had a small television set on top of the cabinets, which we'd turn on to watch the news. That was one of the most exciting, addictive parts of the job: to see the work we'd done just hours before out there in the open. *I was a part of that*, I sometimes thought to myself. But on the day of Helen's Canterbury university visit, all I saw was a disaster. On the screen in front of us, we watched as Helen was surrounded by an unruly crowd, many of whom held nasty banners and handmade signs. Y R U SO UGLY, read one. NICE TEETH, said another. I leaned against a file cabinet, feeling ill.

"Horrible," Grant murmured, eyes fixed on the screen. I nodded, knowing that these images would likely be replayed on repeat.

Helen moved through her speech, struggling to be heard over the jeers. As soon as she finished, she headed toward the car.

Minutes later Grant's phone rang. It was Helen, calling from the road. Grant had just stepped out, but when I told her that, she said, "You'll do." With a level voice far more composed than I'd have been able to muster, she told me she had another event coming up in a few days, this one at Victoria University in Wellington. I was now in charge of making sure it was better managed.

"Okay," I said, hoping I sounded confident though I most definitely was not.

On the day of the Victoria University rally, I arrived on

campus early. I'd barely slept. If this event didn't go well, I knew it would likely mean the end of campus visits. I'd done everything I could, reached out to unions who worked on campus, as well as the young Labour members who had a branch there, but I still worried.

When I arrived, a union leader I knew well was on-site and positioned in the front row with young union delegates, each holding giant white letters. Helen would have a wall around her, a wall that spelled V-O-T-E L-A-B-O-U-R. Soon MPs began to arrive, including one of our ministers, Steve Maharey, a square-jawed former professor. When Helen came into view, right on time, it was to a largely friendly crowd who cheered loudly. As Helen strode to the microphone, she looked relaxed. She was so at ease, in fact, that when a nearly naked protester ran to the front of the crowd, she pointed squarely at him and made a joke. "There's a man up here with no clothes on. It's not very impressive. Quick, someone give me a microscope." The crowd howled.

Okay, I thought. *This is going to be okay.* The only hecklers I could really see—a small group of young men that from their shirts looked like they might be from the youth wing of the National Party—stood at the back, their faces far from the camera, their taunts too far away to be picked up by the microphones.

Still, I watched them through the event. I kept my eyes on

them as they followed behind her, continuing with their heckles right up until she climbed into the car.

I should have ignored them. The event was successful, and besides, they were likely just members of the opposition. It was exactly the kind of thing I should have expected. But my heart was racing, my tiredness mixed with adrenaline was now just becoming anger. As soon as the car pulled out, I stormed over to them. "I can't believe the things you were saying," I snapped. What they were doing wasn't political disagreement. It was nothing but ugly cheap shots. *Don't you know*, I wanted to scream, *how hard it is to do that job? And you just stand in your little scrum, hurling personal insults at people?* But I didn't quite have those words at the ready. I had no impressive monologue. No speech for the ages. Instead, all that spilled off my lips was, "You kiss your mothers with those mouths?"

Steve Maharey, the minister of social development, happened to notice the confrontation, and he made his way over to intervene. As he arrived, one of the hecklers sneered, "Control your *woman*, Steve." The guy's voice dripped with contempt. I was about to bite back when Steve raised his hand.

"Now, now," Steve said, the way a teacher might in a classroom. He stepped between me and the guy, repeating himself. "Now, now. Let's leave it." Then he turned to me. Quietly but firmly, he said, "Come on, Jacinda. It's time to go."

Back at the Beehive, Steve took me aside. *"You can't let them get to you."*

I knew he was right. If I was going to stay in politics, even just an advisory job, I had to learn to keep my cool. But *how*? Everything felt so personal, and I'd never been anything *but* sensitive. How was I supposed to start changing now?

Around that time, Annette King, then the minister of police, met my dad at an event for police officers in Wellington. When she heard Dad's last name, she brightened. "I know your daughter," she said. Then she leaned in and said the thing that people had started saying to me from time to time. "She'd make a great MP."

"Oh, no," Dad responded protectively. "Jacinda's far too thin-skinned for *that*."

Dad wasn't wrong. I *was* thin-skinned. And while I understand it differently today, back then I couldn't see my sensitivity as anything but an obstacle. By then, I knew people who were putting themselves forward to be MPs; one of my roommates had even decided to run for parliament. Sometimes I sat on the couch, listening to him give speeches, offering my feedback and ideas. I knew my input was useful and that my political instincts were strong. And yet there I was in the evenings, sitting on the sofa thinking, *He's so brave.*

All around me, every day, were models of people in politics.

There was Helen, steely, industrious. There was Heather Simpson, intelligent and no-nonsense. There was levelheaded Steve Maharey, and Phil with his intense focus, and Harry with his boundless energy, and not one of them, at least on the face of it, seemed to be "thin-skinned." Sensitivity was my weakness, my tragic flaw, the thing that might just stop me from sticking with the work that I loved.

Soon after Helen won another term in office, I decided to resign. Actually, I decided to leave New Zealand altogether.

I'd been working at the Beehive for more than three years. I'd had three different bosses, three views of what it takes to move government, to lead. Most of the friends I saw regularly were from work. I had no romantic relationship to speak of, no family or kids on the horizon. I had even left the Mormon church when I could no longer reconcile its stance against homosexuality with my strong belief in LGBTQ+ rights. Politics had become my everything, my whole life—so much so that I knew as long as I remained in New Zealand it would stay that way.

"You've got a good job," Dad pressed when I called my parents to tell them I was leaving. "A *really* good job. Why would you leave it?"

Because you were right when you said I'm too thin-skinned. Because while Helen Clark may have shown me that it's possible to be a woman in politics, no one has shown me that you can be sensitive and survive.

I had done my best and worked until my body had broken—the pain in my wrists by now extended up my arms to my shoulders. But all I'd been able to do was to hang on, white-knuckled, to the idea of being a good-enough advisor. Was I running away? Probably. But that was better than staying and facing up to the fact that I couldn't do something.

I booked a ticket to New York City, a place where I had one friend, with one spare couch, and I left.

I had no job, no plan, and it turned out, no idea what was coming.

10

What If You Could Give It Your All

WHEN YOU RUN for parliament, you make a choice: to be out in front, to be the sales rep for big ideas. You'll put yourself forward, ask for votes, say, *Here is why I should be your MP.* You are decisive, confident, ready and willing to step onto the stage.

Perhaps for some people that's how it is. But maybe it's not like that for everyone. Maybe, for you, it happens differently. Maybe the decision unfolds in such tiny increments that it never quite feels like a decision at all. Maybe you even say no at first. Maybe you say no more than once. You can say no as many times as you want. Sometimes it happens anyway.

The first call came on a cold day in late 2007, two years after I left the Beehive. I stood on an icy train platform in South London. I felt the vibration of my phone in my coat pocket. I fished it out, my fingers bright red from the cold, and saw the caller's name: Phil Goff.

Huh. Phil never called me. We hadn't spoken in a year at least.

When I left New Zealand, I'd moved first to New York City. There, I couch surfed with a friend, volunteered at a home care workers' union and a soup kitchen, and drained my savings far faster than I'd expected. That's when I'd packed up and headed to London, where I was eligible to work. As for New Zealand politics, that I had avoided. Mostly.

My conversation with Phil began with small talk. But then he cut to the chase. "Look, we need some young candidates," he said. He was asking me to run in the 2008 election, the next year.

Labour had been suffering from the third-term blues, something that seemed to hit every political party in New Zealand after eight years in office. The National Party, meanwhile, had made significant inroads since the last election. Their new leader, John Key, was a former investment banker who came across as practical and approachable. He had a lot of momentum, and a year out from the election, he had overtaken Labour in the polls by more than ten points.

"We definitely need more young people, and we need more women," Phil continued. "Would you consider coming home? To run?"

In my mind, I was back in the car with Phil in 2002. *If they ever ask you to run*, he'd told me that day, *don't do it*.

I thanked Phil for thinking of me. But I was enjoying my life here in London. Louise lived here now, after splitting with Warren. I was busy, happy, and while I wanted to help the Labour Party, I'd try to find a way to do that from where I was.

The conversation didn't end there, not right away. We went back and forth a little, Phil making a case that there was never a good time to run, but now was better than most, and me deflecting. While he didn't dwell so much on why it was *me* he was asking, the fact he had picked up the phone to call was high praise from Phil.

It was a jolt of confidence. I had left politics behind in New Zealand, but I thought about it all the time. Did I have what it took to run? Let alone withstand the cut and thrust of life in the parliament? No, I didn't think so. But there was a voice in my head I couldn't shake. A voice that said: *What if.*

"Thank you for asking, Phil," I said. "But no thank you."

Months passed. The days grew a tiny bit warmer. I could almost feel the election looming—the tension, the excitement, and my absence—as I took in news from home. I was thousands of miles away, but I craved being a part of it. Then one day, I had an idea to fill the void: *Why don't I bring the campaign here?* I could run a voter enrollment campaign in London, I thought, get New Zealanders living here to vote by mail. After all, to be eligible to vote, you needed only to have stepped foot in New Zealand once in the past three years. I could build a team to help. It might make me feel the way I had during campaigns at home, and even if it didn't, I would at least feel like I was helping.

Then one morning I got another call, this time from Grant. When we'd shared a cramped little office in the Beehive, Grant and I had become good friends. We'd talked about everything—troubleshooting work, my struggles with religion, what we both might do after we left the Beehive.

By early 2008, Grant too had left the Beehive. He was working for the University of Otago. But he'd made the decision to run as the Labour candidate in Wellington Central, a high-profile district in the nation's capital. It would be a tough race, and we'd discussed by phone his decision to run. But in my mind, there was never really any question. Grant was made for parliament.

Now, on the phone, we talked a bit about my London voter enrollment drive, but then he too cut to the chase.

"You know, Jacinda," Grant said. "If you wanted to help Labour from over there, you *could* try to get a spot on the party list."

The party list. I started pacing. *Of course, the party list.*

To understand what Grant was saying, you need to understand the New Zealand electoral system, which is known as mixed-member proportional (MMP). In MMP, each voter gets two votes: an electorate vote and a party vote. The electorate vote is straightforward: You vote for whichever candidate you'd like to see represent your local area in parliament. The candidate who wins the majority of votes wins that seat. Most of the seats in parliament—72 of 120—are filled this way.

With your party vote, on the other hand, you vote for whichever political *party* you'd like to see form a government. Most of the time, a voter gives their party vote to their preferred candidate's party. In New Plymouth, for example, that meant a vote for Harry and then a vote for Labour. On election night, all the votes are tallied. If a party gets a greater share of the party vote than the seats they gained through electorate votes, then they will get a "top up"—some extra MPs drawn from a party's list—the very thing for which Grant was encouraging me to put my name forward.

The list contained the full roster of potential MPs, ranked in descending order. Your party leader—for Labour, that was Helen Clark—is number one on the list. The leader is followed by the heavy hitters, mostly existing MPs, with a few bright new prospects sprinkled in between, all the way through to almost every candidate running in a seat and some who aren't. Being on the list didn't mean you'd be an MP—there were more people on it than there were winnable seats—but it was a great way to support the party.

My voter enrollment campaign had almost everything it needed, except for one thing: a platform. Maybe if I could call myself an actual candidate, rather than just some random person trying to register voters, I could get a bit more media attention.

It was like Grant was reading my mind too. "Being a candidate will probably help your enrollment drive," he said into the phone. Even from this distance, nearly twelve thousand miles away, he knew how to convince me of something.

And I could just picture him, pacing around his living room, adjusting his problematic back, his eyebrows rising playfully as he delivered the clincher.

"I think it could really help the party, Jacinda."

I held my breath for a few seconds, trying to figure out if what I felt was nerves, or excitement.

"Huh," I finally said. "Maybe I will."

Maybe when you run for parliament, you convince yourself you're not *actually* running. A spot on the list will help your *real* cause: helping Labour win. That's the only reason you're doing this. To help the party. Not to become an MP.

At home before bed, you ask your sister to take a headshot of you. You print out the forms, and you fill them out, writing your name down carefully, clearly, in large, firm block letters. Your insides squirm as you check the box: Party Candidate. Then you sign the form with big cursive script that is so illegible it could really be anyone's name. But it's yours.

You scan it all and send it off. Then you turn out the light and lie in the dark not sleeping. You've said no so many times, but maybe you just said yes.

After that, things moved quickly. I flew to Wellington for the regional list conference, where the local party list is created and ranked. It was odd being back, as if two years hadn't even passed. Mum and Dad joined me, and as we walked together across the gravel parking lot, I described what was about to happen. It would be a bit like speed dating, actually. I and dozens of other candidates, including Grant, would introduce ourselves to small groups of local Labour members, answer questions, and share our vision for the party. We'd each be ranked regionally, then in a few weeks, the national committee would merge all the regional lists into one, with numerical rankings given to everyone.

While my mum was cheerful and supportive, my dad was a lot less sure. "Is running for something you won't win such a good idea?" Dad asked, frowning. I explained my reasoning. That it might help with our campaign in London, and that getting out the party vote there was important. Especially with tight races like Wellington Central—the one Grant was running in.

We stepped into the musty hall, the kind used for Boy Scout meetings. Walking in, I nodded hello at familiar faces—people I recognized from working on campaigns or alongside the unions. Inside, stackable seats lined up facing the front. I stood at the back of the room, scanning the crowd until I saw Grant. Technically, we were competitors. But there was no one I wanted to see in parliament more than Grant. He was progressive, smart, funny, and kind. If Grant didn't win his race, a good spot on the list would be his ticket to parliament. As far as I was concerned, this was Grant's day.

When the time came, I moved between groups, cheerfully telling them about myself and answering questions.

Hi, I'm Jacinda, I'm working on an enrollment campaign in London.

Why am I here? I've been a party member and volunteer in campaigns for years, just like you. I want to help Labour win . . .

With the speed dating done, we reassembled into one large

group for the ranking process to begin. I sat in with Mum and Dad as I watched MPs be nominated.

At first it was all quick, a formality of ranking existing MPs. Then the first new opening came up.

"Nominations?" Silence fell over the room. A member of Grant's team stood and yelled, "GRANT ROBERTSON." I waited a beat for the seconder to stand. Instead, it was Grant who stood.

"I don't wish to be ranked," Grant said. "Not until Jacinda Ardern has been." He flashed me a smile, the kind that says *I know exactly what I just did*, and then turned his eyes back to the front. I sat silently in the room, watching all the process hum around me. Someone nominated me, another seconded my name, and with that, I was added to the list. Grant had just guaranteed that I would be ranked higher than him. That act could be the difference between him being in parliament and not. It was, to this day, one of the most selfless, generous political acts I've ever seen.

And it also nudged me closer to landing in parliament.

When you run for parliament, you wait. Wait for the campaign to start. Wait for the flyers to arrive. Wait till you can put signs up. Wait for someone to answer the door. Wait to find out whether people will choose you, or first, whether your party will.

But sometimes, deep down, you already know.

By the time the national committee met to merge all of the regional lists, I was back in my apartment in London. It was five a.m. when my phone burst into life.

"Mate," said a husky voice on the other end of the line. It was my friend Tolley, the union leader who'd helped me plan that university visit for Helen Clark, the one where I'd lost my cool.

"You're number twenty, mate. You're number twenty."

Number twenty? That meant that the party had ranked me above sitting MPs.

I knew I had ideas. I had worked hard in the party, had built good networks, and was as committed to getting Labour elected as anyone. And yet I was still surprised.

I sat up in bed. My room was dark and quiet, my roommates asleep in the rooms above me. In the last election, Labour had won fifty seats. Since becoming an MMP system, Labour had never won fewer than thirty-seven.

No matter what happened on election day, it was virtually guaranteed: I would be going into parliament.

But of course, that wasn't the end of things, not by a long shot. Within a few weeks, I'd learn that the Labour Party didn't have a candidate in my old hometown of Morrinsville. And no wonder; it was an unwinnable seat. They'd been hunting around to find someone who would put their name on the ballot in the place where I'd grown up. I was on the party list, almost guaranteed to be going to parliament, but I was still able to run in a district. Almost everyone on the party list did.

The answer was obvious: I would run the unwinnable race in my hometown.

I packed my London apartment into boxes. My plan to stay in London to campaign, and my time overseas, was coming to an end. I was going home.

The booing didn't start off loudly. It began as a hum—a gentle chord from a relatively small number of people—the early adopters, if you will. At first, the sound of it seemed almost like background noise. But then others joined in. Then more. Before long it became a glorious chorus of utter disdain.

I was at my first candidate meeting, and things weren't going well. About fifty people had gathered in Matamata, twenty minutes from Morrinsville, in a community room with a low ceiling and padded chairs. The moderator was from a farming lobby called the Federated Farmers, and most of the room leaned conservative.

Each time the National Party candidate spoke, I could see the whole room nodding, as well as eyes lighting up. Then it was my turn. The question was about climate change. I don't remember the exact wording, but I remember the implication: Did I "believe" in it?

As soon as I'd started to answer, I saw arms fold, heads shake. Smiles morphed into suspicious glares. My eyes flicked to the rear of the room. My mother sat up straight in her chair, beaming at me, as if her warmth alone could make up for everyone else's hostility. Next to her sat my grandma Margaret, a slight look of skepticism from behind her large rectangular glasses. The edges of her mouth turned downward, the shape of displeasure.

A few weeks prior, my grandmother had lent me her car to go door-knocking. She'd worn that same expression as she watched Granddad Eric, who kindly and carefully helped me mount a set of speakers and Labour signs on the car roof. When a neighbor walked by, Grandma Margaret yelled loudly and clearly, "The things you do for your grandchildren!" Lest there be any doubt about her political affiliation.

My grandmother was not a Labour supporter, not at all. But as I answered the question about climate change, at least she wasn't booing me, like the other attendees. I kept my eyes on her for one more beat. At least I didn't *think* my grandmother was booing me.

I care deeply about the issue of climate change. The Māori concept of kaitiakitanga, that we are all guardians of the land, the sea, and the sky, feels very real to me. I still remember learning about the hole in the ozone layer as a child. The problem was caused by something called chlorofluorocarbons: human-made chemicals found in aerosol sprays, solvents, air conditioners, and refrigerators, which were broken down by the sun's rays and released atoms that destroyed ozone. By virtue of where we sat on the globe, New Zealand had less protection from the sun than most places.

My child mind connected the dots. *People around the world use hair spray, and so now I have to wear more sunscreen?* It was the first time I understood that not only do humans affect our planet, but our choices affect one another, even when we're thousands of miles apart. Now, with the climate crisis, we were seeing this dynamic on a massive scale. Here in New Zealand, rising sea levels due to climate change threatened our coastlines, our low-lying areas, and islands in the Pacific Ocean that were our neighbors.

Labour had recently created an emissions trading scheme, a way to price greenhouse gases with the ultimate goal of reducing emissions, but it hadn't gone through without a fight. In rural communities like Matamata, there was concern that agricultural emissions, which primarily came from cows releasing the greenhouse gas methane when they burped, might one day be included in this scheme. Some thought this unfair; others refused to believe methane was part of the problem at all. A few had even driven their tractors to the Beehive to make the point, with one National Party MP maneuvering a rusty, muddy-looking tractor up the stairs of parliament. His name was Shane Ardern, and he was a distant cousin to me (*by marriage*, as Aunty Marie always reminded me).

But I believed the issue was too important, and if we were to live by the idea of kaitiakitanga, we needed to be frank about what tackling climate change would mean. Even if it meant a ripple of discomfort moving through this room in the form of very audible booing.

After the event ended—after the tepid applause, and after I'd shaken hands with my opponents, and after a seething older man with black strands of hair combed over his bald head jammed a finger in my face and called me a communist—I approached my mum and grandmother. Mum smiled encouragingly and patted me on the shoulder.

"Well done!" my mother said.

"Thanks, Mum. But I'm not sure it went *that* well."

"What made you think it was bad?" she asked as if we had been in two totally different rooms.

"Ahh . . . the booing?" I said.

She waved her hands dismissively. "I wouldn't worry about that."

I turned to Grandma Margaret. "And what did you think, Grandma?"

She glanced around the room, craning her neck. "I thought the candidate for New Zealand First was wonderful," she said. She meant Barbara Stewart, a woman in her fifties with a large black-and-white rosette pinned to her chest. She turned and looked at me hopefully. "Can you introduce me to her?"

That's when it occurred to me. Even my grandmother might not vote for me.

After a few too many bad events, you'll talk to an MP, someone you like and call a friend. You'll tell him about the booing, and he'll shrug. "Eh," he'll say, "if fifty percent of a room isn't disagreeing with you, you probably aren't saying anything anyway."

You'll remind yourself of that often—like every time someone flips you off. And that will happen a lot.

I wasn't going to win the electorate vote. That was almost certain, since the electorate in my district of Morrinsville was far too conservative for *any* Labour candidate. Yet I knew that because of my place on the party list, I'd almost certainly end up in parliament.

But that didn't stop me from campaigning like the election depended on it.

I channeled every door-knocking technique I had learned in New Plymouth, rattling gates, knocking on the doors of areas where I knew there were Labour voters not once, but several times. I filled out endless enrollment forms alongside first-time voters and drove out to the farthest-flung corners of the district where we had no volunteers to hand-deliver flyers. I gave it everything I had.

And after four weeks phone-banking, visiting local businesses, and waving campaign signs along rural roads, election day arrived. Labour had been trailing in all of the recent polls. The idea of winning felt less and less likely.

On election night, I put on a red dress I had bought a few weeks earlier and a pair of black Mary Jane heels. My mum, Marie, and I climbed into Mum's car and drove to the Taniwharau League club in Huntly—a big space with a bar at the back and Labour signs leaning against the wall. There, we sat at a small round table watching results roll in on a large screen that usually projected rugby games. Among the patrons in track pants and rugby league shirts, I felt wildly overdressed.

When my numbers flashed up, they only confirmed what we all already expected: I had not won the rural conservative seat in which I'd grown up; I would have to rely on the party list. Though, there was one glimmer of joy that evening: Grant had won the Wellington Central seat.

But the night's disappointments weren't over yet. Before long, Harry's numbers came in showing he had lost the New Plymouth seat by 105 votes. Next to me, Marie began to sob. That's when we left.

We were driving home in the dark, Mum nodding off next to me and Marie weeping in the back seat, when Helen Clark arrived at the Labour Party's election night headquarters, conceded defeat to John Key of the National Party, and resigned.

Labour had lost government. The conservative National Party would be in charge. I thought about all that Labour had accomplished, and all that might be undone.

But Labour had gotten 34 percent of the party vote—more than enough to guarantee me a spot in parliament. I would be an MP.

When you're sworn into parliament, the experience might be bittersweet. Maybe you're in opposition, watching a party that isn't your own take the helm of government. MPs you admired, maybe even worked for, may no longer be there, the formal nameplates on their doors removed and replaced with new names. All the things you had wanted to do and wanted to change would have to wait—until when, it's hard to know.

And yet one morning in November, you wake early. You dress in a black blazer, carefully clipping a bracelet that had once belonged to your nana, gold-plated with a bamboo motif, onto your wrist. And a few hours later you get to cross the threshold from the "ayes or nos" lobby into the debating chamber with its high ceilings, wood panels, and green leather chairs. You sit down in one of those chairs. And when you hear your name called, and you cross the debating chamber floor, raise your hand, and are sworn in, it will still feel joyful.

It might even feel like the honor of a lifetime.

11

What If You Could Keep Going

I HADN'T BEEN in office long before I was properly heckled for an outrageous offense: I had stood to speak from the wrong seat. While the debating chamber might appear stately, it can also feel like a fighting ring for a very uncool rap battle—complete with insults, jeers, and taunts. This wasn't like when I was booed while campaigning in Matamata. Booing, after all, is a generalized kind of noise that you can tune out. This was different. I was being jeered loudly and audibly by fellow MPs from the other party, with words I could make out with painful clarity.

I was still speaking, but I could barely hear myself. I didn't want my internal quiver to become an external shake. I didn't want them to see how inexperienced I felt, how *silly*. So

I masked my shame with volume, speaking louder and louder, as if the loudness of my voice would substitute for the strength I did not feel. Then I returned to my own seat, internally criticizing myself, my dad's words ringing in my ears: *too thin-skinned* for parliament.

I wasn't naive. I knew that the job came with snide comments from other politicians, casual insults from the public, and the sad but simple fact that anyone who stands in any spotlight can and will attract haters. I knew these things came with the territory. But now I was learning firsthand how it felt. And it felt brutal.

My options to fix the problem were limited. I was a new MP with almost no influence. I couldn't change the rules. I certainly couldn't change the culture. So instead, I thought about changing myself. And I knew exactly who to ask for help, a fellow Labour MP infamous for being a bruiser: Trevor Mallard.

I didn't really know Trevor, but I'd seen him when I worked for Helen Clark's office—usually because he was in some kind of trouble. He had the physique of a high school rugby coach and was bullish, impulsive, and blunt—a partisan attack dog who inspired fury in his enemies and sometimes exasperation among his friends. On one occasion, during an intense debate in the chamber, a member of the opposition made an insulting remark about Trevor's family. At the end of the session, Trevor gestured to the MP to "come outside" and, after a tense verbal argument in the lobby, whacked him.

A few days after my mistake in the debating chamber, I chased down Trevor in the hallway. I recounted my error, then said flatly, "I need to toughen up." I told him that if I didn't start caring less about what people said to me, and about me, this job was going to be too hard. And as the toughest, least sensitive person I knew, could he help me?

Trevor stopped walking and turned to face me. As he listened, his face registered surprise, then he furrowed his brow. "Jacinda, is that how you see me?"

Was he joking? That's the way *everyone* saw him. I smiled, assuming this was obvious.

Trevor glanced away for a moment. Then he leaned in. In a quiet, clear voice, he said, "Promise me you won't try to toughen up, Jacinda. You feel things because you have empathy and because you care. The moment you change that is the moment you'll stop being good at your job." And with that, Trevor gave me a reassuring smile and strode off down the hall.

The next nine years were not easy for the Labour Party as we saw our popularity and support plummet with each successive year. As a member of parliament, I did as much media as I could to get the word out about policies we hoped would improve people's lives. I promoted our tax credit for families with children, as well as the laws I'd drafted to combat child poverty. I wanted to understand what was happening in state-run foster care, so I read years' worth of coroners' reports for children who had died while they were meant to be under the protection of government agencies, talked to experts, and tried to identify where the system was breaking down for kids.

But if I was intent on centering ideas, my opponents were much more concerned with appearances, and they took me on, literally, from head to toe; I was urged to dye my hair, fix my teeth, change my shoes. A persistent refrain began to pop up about me. It came from commentators in the media mostly, intentional insults in articles or opinion pieces. They said I had made "no important contribution in [my] portfolio work," and that "pretty faces get you only so far." I was called vapid, vacant, even "pretty bloody stupid." The criticism was so common that sometimes I found the words echoing in my own head. What *had* I accomplished?

It is different for women in the public eye. It is different for women, period. I felt that so acutely every time I went on television. Maybe that's why, when I got a call from the editor of a woman's magazine asking if I would appear in a series on body image, a piece to empower women, I said yes. Here was a chance to talk about how it felt to be seeing yourself constantly through the eyes of others, comparing yourself to some unspoken, impossible standard: We can be ourselves, but not show too much of ourselves. Be comfortable, but never dowdy. Dress smart, but not too fancy. Being in the public eye had made me more self-conscious, but perhaps it had also made me more determined to acknowledge that the additional judgment women faced was unfair. So the answer was yes, I would be happy to talk about body image with women all over New Zealand.

"Great," the editor said. "So for the accompanying photo, we'd like you to wear either a swimsuit or shapewear."

Shapewear? "You know," she said. "Like Spanx?"

Wait, I thought. *I didn't know this was a show-and-tell situation. You want me to be photographed in Spanx for a magazine that will sit in doctors' offices, and in supermarkets, and on the small table next to my grandmother's chair?*

I could have said no. In fact, I very nearly did. But instead, a few weeks later I found myself in front of a camera wearing three-quarter-length shapewear, while a stranger aimed a blow-dryer at my face to create a windswept effect in my puffed-up, overly styled hair.

I doubt it made any difference to the women of New Zealand to see a sitting MP wearing Spanx. But if there was even the chance that it might have made just one person think less about the way they look and more about their ability to do a job, then I was happy to have done it. After all, I had a platform. It may have been small, it may have meant putting myself into a humiliating situation from time to time, but it was something.

Nearly every day I was reminded why I stuck around in opposition, why I put up with being criticized for my looks and subjected to taunts from fellow MPs: *because it made a difference.* Yes, some days were a grind. But there was always something to get you out of bed in the morning.

Sometimes, we could stop things we opposed, like the time we managed to put an end to the government's plan to mine in conservation areas. Or you might draft bills like the one I had put forward requiring the government to track child poverty and offer a plan to reduce it. Sometimes those bills were voted on, like the one I'd written to modernize adoption laws. And every day—every single day as an MP—I came across individuals I could help.

Early on, I met a grandmother raising her grandchild who had shaken baby syndrome. Music therapy helped, but the government had cut her funding for it. I was able to help get it restored. Then there was the business owner who explained that a quirk of New Zealand law meant that when they added a New Zealand censorship rating to a DVD or CD, they had to put it *beneath* the clear wrapper and not on top of it. This meant it cost extra time and money to reseal the packages. I was able to get the law changed, to fix it. It was so small, but it helped someone.

There was always some tiny thing you could do for people, and the tiny things added up to a feeling of usefulness. And more often than not, that was enough to carry me forward, to keep me going, even on the hardest days. And with loss after loss for Labour, election after election, there were plenty of those.

Another thing that got me through those hard days was meeting Clarke Gayford, a TV host and DJ, but someone who probably preferred to be called a seafarer or fisherman.

It took a while for us to become an official couple. And it was a bit like the first time I had run for parliament: one step, then another, each so incrementally small there was no clear moment that it happened. Was it discovering we both loved the black petrel and were cheering for it to win the fiercely competitive if quaint-sounding "New Zealand Bird of the Year" battle? Was it the trip to Waiheke Island? The time we had lunch and he gave my knee a gentle squeeze under the table? Or the first time he took me to his sister's for dinner and we ate with his nieces perched in high chairs next to us? All I know is that one day, when things had been especially tough in parliament, Clarke suggested I take a few hours off in the afternoon. "It's a beautiful day," he said, "perfect for some time on the sea. It will be good for you."

Clarke was so different from the people I knew in politics. He was uninhibited and unself-conscious, and yet at times, also shy and often self-contained. Politics is all about appealing to other people. Nearly everyone I worked with thought constantly about polling, messaging, connecting with voters. But Clarke? He was just completely himself.

I met him at his apartment and jumped into his Jeep as he pulled his boat trailer the short distance down to the harbor. I stood on the jetty, holding ropes as he winched the boat into the water.

Moments later we were gliding across a perfectly still ocean, heading to a spot where Clarke was sure there would be snapper biting, when his arm excitedly shot into the air. I followed where he was pointing, just in time to see a silhouette across the sky. A black petrel.

I don't know what it was about that moment exactly, but I knew then. There was no "me and my friend Clarke" anymore. There was just "us."

In February 2017, due to a special election to fill an unexpected vacancy in the Mount Albert district, I won a seat as an electorate MP with my very own constituency. I had run and lost several races to become an electorate MP over the last few election cycles, and now, finally, I was no longer just a list MP. Not that there was any time to celebrate.

It was still an election year for the full parliament. Voters would go to the polls in just seven months. And our party leader, Andrew Little, selected me to be his deputy, though I did not feel entirely ready for the job. I was thirty-six years old; Annette King, a friend and mentor who had most recently held the number two spot, had served in parliament for thirty-three years. And the recent commentary when I took over the role of deputy didn't help either. A senior journalist wrote in *The New Zealand Herald*, on March 3, 2017: ". . . so, Andrew Little has landed himself a show pony in Jacinda Ardern."

Oh. This again.

I was asked to respond to this commentary, some variation of which I had encountered regularly for nearly a decade. Even a member of my own party had suggested that me being promoted might be seen as a token gesture. If I spoke out against these taunts, I knew I'd be portrayed as humorless and too sensitive. And then *that* would become the story. The trick, I figured, was to respond with a jokey nonanswer that would take the story nowhere, even if that meant doing nothing for women in politics. So, like I had on countless occasions, I said very little, instead throwing myself into the role and using my first official speech as deputy to talk about mental health for young people and the things that kept me in politics.

Inside, though, I began to notice that something had changed when I heard comments like this. After over eight years in parliament, the shock of them had worn off. Now that they no longer surprised me, I saw that instead of contributing to my self-doubt, they had begun to have the opposite effect. These insults acted as a counterweight to my impostor syndrome. Did I still doubt myself? Absolutely. But my own doubt was one thing. Hearing it publicly from others was something else entirely. I could hear and feel how wrong their words were, in a way I'd never been able to when they came from within me. I *wasn't* shallow; I *wasn't* empty. And now I was determined to prove it.

Labour's popularity continued to crater over the course of 2017. The polls hadn't been great for a long time, but the last couple of polls had been surprisingly grim. By August we were polling at 23 percent, while the National Party was at 42 percent. We weren't just looking at election defeat, we were looking at annihilation—the prospect of losing so many MPs that Labour, with its one-hundred-year history, could eventually cease to be a credible major party. I kept pinning our hopes on the start of the campaign, in just a few weeks, to give us the platform we needed. **Regardless of how those polls bounce around**, I texted Andrew after seeing the latest results, **I will always be an optimist for us. Things will get better!**

But when he replied, it was only to tell me he wanted to talk.

Andrew's office was always cold, and as I walked in the chilled air made me shudder. Andrew stood behind his large wooden desk, staring past me as if lost in thought. I made my way to the couch and sat down, waiting to hear what he needed from me.

Andrew cleared his throat. "I think I should stand down," he said. "And I think you should take over as leader."

I could hear voices in the hallway, the bustle of MPs getting ready to go to the house. Doors opening and closing. The whir of a printer. I turned his words over in my head, tried to make them make sense. *Andrew wants to stand down. He thinks I should take over.*

I wasn't naive. I knew people considered me a potential leader. Just weeks earlier, a magazine had run a cover story with the headline *Jacinda Ardern: Why She Is Our Prime Minister in Waiting.* I had even started showing up in the preferred prime minister polls, albeit with a paltry 8 percent.

But I had also been in politics long enough to know that commentators touted MPs as future leaders all the time. It was one thing to hear people speculate. But this was less than two months before an election. We had already filmed ads and put up giant billboards as a team, with me as Andrew's number two.

I sat in stunned silence while Andrew explained that perhaps it would be in the best interest of the party. He didn't think he could win. If he were to stay on, he reasoned, we'd lose too many MPs.

Even as he spoke, some part of my mind was already racing ahead, weeks into a hypothetical future.

The debates, I thought. The televised debates against the current prime minister, Bill English. *I can't do them. I can't do any of it.*

And that was another reason that all of the public speculation about my becoming leader was wrong. None of the people who wrote those headlines, or who answered those poll questions, knew what I knew: that if my immediate thought when asked to pick up the baton was to begin listing all the reasons why I couldn't, then I was not strong enough to lead.

I don't know what Andrew was saying when I finally interrupted him. But I remember I spoke clearly and concisely. With a firm voice, I explained to him why change right now was a bad idea. We needed stability. The party needed it. The voters needed it. We could pull our numbers back up when the campaign started. I was mid-sentence when the bells began to chime, calling members of parliament into the debating chamber. I stood up and prepared to head downstairs.

"We'll talk again?" I asked.

In response, Andrew simply nodded. I couldn't tell if I'd convinced him that he needed to stay, or if I'd only convinced myself.

Six days later, I walked into the Legislative Council Chamber, where twenty members of the media were gathered and waiting. The microphones were on, the cameras rolling. I took my place in front of the microphones. Next to me stood Kelvin Davis, a former school principal, the MP for Te Tai Tokerau and our newly elected deputy leader. Kelvin was a man of quiet mana with rural roots whom Grant had nominated as deputy and the caucus unanimously backed. Grant stood behind me, and other top members of Labour flanked my sides. I was wearing a black dress, bright red blazer, bright red lipstick. The colors of Labour.

"Thank you, everyone, for joining us this afternoon," I said. "I want to start by giving a brief statement." Flashbulbs popped, and I could hear the camera shutters clicking.

"Following Andrew's announcement this morning," I continued, "I was nominated to be leader of the Labour Party. My nomination was unanimously accepted."

I'd been deputy leader for exactly five months. Now, I was running to be the prime minister of New Zealand. There were moments where I hovered above myself, just an observer to these high-speed events. It all felt so surreal.

It had been six days since Andrew had called me into his office and questioned whether he could go on as leader. Soon after, another dismal poll was taken. The pressure increased. In the days that followed, I still wasn't clear what Andrew was thinking, but in the back of my mind I began to let the "what if" scenarios play out. *IF he went, what would I say? IF I was nominated, what would I do? IF I was leader, what would the campaign need to look like?*

And now here I was. Andrew had resigned. I was now the Labour leader. And the election was just fifty-three days away.

I continued my statement, using the trick I'd figured out years before: that if I spoke loudly and forcefully, I could keep my voice from shaking. I used words like *resolve, steadfast, determined.* I shared Labour's vision for New Zealand: that our country be a place where everyone has a roof over their head and meaningful work, where education is free, where children live surrounded by creativity, not poverty, where we lead the world on environmental issues. I wanted, in other words, to put into practice kaitiakitanga—to build a New Zealand even better than the way we found it. I said that Kelvin and I would be positive, organized, and ready for the election—as if there weren't, at this very moment, hundreds of billboards across the country featuring the face of someone who was no longer party leader.

And then I took questions. They came quickly.

Do you think you are up to the job of prime minister?

What do you believe equips you for that?

Do you believe you can credibly form a government with [polling at just] 24 percent?

Who are *Jacinda Ardern and Kelvin Davis?*

As I answered, I held my head up. Tried to project the confidence that I didn't quite feel as I heard the questions I was being asked. And then it was over. It was fast and for the most part upbeat—twenty-five minutes all told—and the best start I could have given us.

But nothing about this was going to be easy.

The next fifty-three days were a whirlwind: intense, grueling, inspiring, demanding. Day in and day out, I traveled around New Zealand, trying to cover an entire 103,475-square-mile country in a matter of weeks, meeting as many voters as possible, while also reorienting our campaign strategy, staying on top of every issue that arose, and producing our new policy agenda. TV appearances began immediately too, and so did questions about my biological clock. I was now thirty-seven years old, and while Clarke and I had wanted to have a baby, we had not been successful. It was painful for me; I had always assumed I would be a mum, but my body was not complying. So while I did not share my private struggles with the world, that didn't stop people from wondering.

When reporter after reporter asked me if I was pregnant, what would happen if I became pregnant, if I wanted to have a baby, I gave the best response I could. "My position is no different to the woman who works three jobs, or who might be in a position where they are juggling lots of responsibilities." Another nonanswer, this one a balancing act of unknowns: the impact of my hypothetical pregnancy on my hypothetical election as prime minister.

But one day, I was preparing to go on a morning show when Mark Richardson, the man who read the sports news, said I should be open about my reproductive plans.

"If you are the employer of a company," he said, "you need to know that type of thing from the woman you are employing . . . the question is, is it okay for the prime minister to take maternity leave while in office?"

When it was my time to go on the air, I took my seat opposite the hosts. I had no specific plan in mind, but Mark's comment angered me. It was one thing to talk about me, but he'd framed the discussion as if *every* woman of childbearing age was obliged to share their reproductive plans—and not so the potential employer could prepare a gift basket, but presumably so they could decide whether she was worth hiring.

When the moment came, I said: "Yes, I had talked openly in the past about wanting to be a mother. I decided to talk about it, it was my choice, so that means I am happy to keep responding to those questions."

Then I turned to Mark Richardson and extended my index finger toward him. "But *you*," I said. "It is totally unacceptable in 2017 to say that women should have to answer that question in the workplace, *it is unacceptable*." The lone woman co-host began to applaud as I doubled down. All of the times when I had said nothing, where I chose silence for fear of appearing humorless—it all suddenly came crashing through to the surface as I repeated the words a third time. "It is *unacceptable*."

Back in the car, heading to the airport, my press secretary Mike Jaspers took out his phone. A wry smile filled his face as he showed me his screen. Someone had already made a meme of the moment: me, with my finger extended, my eyebrows raised, with text added in bold typeface: **JACINDA ARDERN HAS NO TIME FOR YOUR [CRAP].**

The day before the election, Clarke and I arrived at St. David's Church in Te Aroha. My grandma Margaret had just passed away. She had fallen ill a few weeks prior, but the suddenness of it all shocked me. As we stepped out of the car, I spotted a photographer holding up a camera. I nodded a silent greeting in their direction. *Must be hard,* I thought, *being dispatched to take a photo of someone at their grandmother's funeral.*

I'd barely gotten to see Grandma Margaret one last time. She'd had two strokes, and by the time I had gotten to the hospital, my family was gathered around her. They spoke quietly as she lay still, eyes shut. Granddad Eric sat to her side. He had softened as he'd gotten older, become gentler, and now was holding my grandmother's hand. I moved to the side of the bed, wrapping my arms around her, whispering my name so that she knew I was there.

My grandmother had always seen the world differently than I did. We disagreed on almost everything: civil unions, the welfare system, immigration. She had voted conservatively her whole life, and proudly so.

I knew my grandmother loved me. But I thought my political leanings had been something she'd endured. At best, she'd tolerated them. At worst, they embarrassed her. And still, in that hospital room, after I moved toward her and whispered my name, she said her five final words to me: *I am proud of you.*

After the funeral, I spied Grant, who to my surprise had flown up. I was making my way toward him when a congregant, a woman my mother's age I didn't recognize, made a beeline for me. "Jacinda," the woman said. "I just wanted to tell you that there are a lot of people in Morrinsville who are praying for you."

I smiled. "Thank you," I said. "That is so kind."

She took my two hands in hers, pressed them tight. "They're not *voting* for you," she clarified, "but they *are* praying for you."

On election night, September 23, 2017, and in the weeks that followed, the votes were tabulated. Labour had made huge gains over the course of the campaign, overcoming those tough polls from just fifty-three days prior. Now, in combination with the Green Party, we had won enough votes to form a government on one condition: if New Zealand First, the small party headed by Winston Peters, agreed to join our coalition. So we started a series of negotiations with them, but so did the National Party. Whichever party New Zealand First agreed to work with would lead the government. I had no idea who they were going to pick.

As these talks were ongoing, a very different sort of result came in. One night I went to my friend Julia's for dinner. Julia was younger than me but also maternalistic, with a background in public health. Our conversations always started with her asking me the same question: "How are you feeling?" Earlier that day, when I told her that I didn't feel quite right and described a few unusual symptoms, she had gone out and bought a pregnancy test. At the end of dinner, she pulled it out of a shopping bag like it was an after-dinner mint.

"Just in case," she said. I brought it with me into her bathroom and took the test.

The stick showed double lines. Positive. I was pregnant.

"Juliaaa!"

I had gone through endless testing, multiple failed medical interventions. I'd been told that my constant work, my lifestyle, the stress of it all, would keep me from having a baby. Now here I was, in the middle of trying to become prime minister, and I was pregnant. My mind reeled. Now?! This was happening now?! I slumped onto the bathroom floor.

"One foot in front of the other," Julia said when she saw the positive result. She patted me on the shoulder. "One foot in front of the other." I had to just keep going. Julia left me alone in the bathroom, closing the door behind her. I pulled myself up onto the toilet and called Clarke.

A few days later, Winston Peters was ready to make an announcement about New Zealand First's decision. There had been no phone call from Winston, and I had absolutely no idea what would happen next. My team assembled in my office on the third floor of parliament to watch it on television. Clarke stood nearby, dressed more formally than usual. Annette, Kelvin, and Grant were there, of course, as well as the protection officers assigned to me for the campaign, and about a dozen other senior party leaders and staff.

As we waited in my office for the press conference to begin, the television was on but muted. Annette sat on the couch, her eyes darting between me and the screen in front of us. Behind her, Grant stood anxiously, palms together at his forehead as if in prayer, rocking back and forth. We were waiting. Waiting for cameras to flick from the studio, live to the Beehive. Waiting for Winston to emerge from his office. Waiting to know what the future held.

There had been so much waiting. Waiting for this conference. Waiting through every day of the negotiation. Waiting for vote results, waiting for polls, waiting through years and years in opposition for the chance to *do* something. In a few minutes, the waiting would end, and either I would be back in opposition or I would be the prime minister of New Zealand.

And then a sudden flurry. "Turn it up!" Winston Peters was on the screen.

For the first few minutes, Winston spoke in general terms, no hint of what he'd chosen. His face was that of a man at a poker match: intense concentration, giving nothing away. My breath felt caught in my throat. Then he said it: *We have chosen Labour.*

The room erupted in celebration. I could hear the cheers around me and echoing up and down the hallway. But for me, everything briefly went quiet. I stared at the screen, taking in what he'd said. *New Zealand First had chosen us.*

I was meant to save the party from a crushing defeat, to lift our numbers out of the gutter. I had felt so responsible—for my colleagues, our staff—but most of all, for the people who needed us to win. It was a pressure that I had tried to suppress, so that every day I could get up and keep going. But now, it was like a lid had been lifted. All the pressure, the worry, and fear were rushing out of my body. What was left felt like relief and pure joy.

We did it.

I did it.

I would be prime minister of New Zealand.

Grant threw his arms around me and began to shake with loud happy sobs. Clarke, who had watched the announcement from the corner of the room, came and wrapped his arms around me. Then someone, I don't know who, shoved a whiskey into my hand. I looked down at the cut glass tumbler and then set the glass down.

Yes, I was the prime minister.

And I was also pregnant.

12

What If You Could Be Kind

I COULD TELL you about my swearing in. I could tell you about the dress that I wore, a red-and-blue knee-length number in brocade fabric. Or about the bus, the one I rode with newly minted cabinet ministers from the small ceremony at Government House back to parliament. I could explain that stepping off the bus, we heard saxophones, a trombone, a steady percussive beat; a handful of members from an iconic Wellington band, Fat Freddy's Drop, was playing exuberantly at the base of the Parliament House steps.

I could tell you about the crowds that day: lining the forecourt, pressing up against the perimeter fencing, against each other. People in suits and T-shirts, scarves and sunglasses, head coverings and baseball caps, a riot of color beneath a bright blue October sky.

I could tell you about the formal events: speeches, the signing of the warrants, and being positioned for official photos like we were back in school. What it was like looking behind me from the table at the swearing-in ceremony to see my dad in his suit, sitting next to Clarke in his suit. Dad was sneaking texts with my mum, who was in London with Louise, who'd just given birth to a baby boy named Alejandro. Then, walking into parliament hand in hand with Clarke and his nieces, the ones who'd sat in high chairs when I'd first met his family—the older girl in Converse sneakers, the younger with her braids askew.

There is so much I could tell you about that day, but it all felt a bit like a blur, a beautiful whirl of smiles and handshakes and hugs, the cool air blowing through the bus windows.

So, I will tell you instead about a conversation I had just before it all began. I was in the car, en route to Government House, where I would officially take office. I was on the phone, speaking with John Campbell, a journalist I'd been watching since I was eleven years old. John wanted to catch me in the final quiet moments before everything changed.

He asked how I was doing, and I answered, like it were any other day, "I'm well, thank you. How are you?"

"Well, I'm good," he said, amused. "But I mean, I'm not driving to Government House to become the prime minister." Then he asked me where I was, and I told him I was next to a Subway sandwich shop. A set of jackhammers started up as we rounded the bend from Aitken to Mulgrave Street and passed our national archives.

"And when you return," he said, "the next time you're back in parliament, you will be the fortieth prime minister of New Zealand. It's an extraordinary thing, isn't it?"

Well, yes. I suppose it was.

John asked me for "one last idealistic flourish" before the hard work of governing began. "Untethered, big-picture stuff. What is it you want to do?"

I had answered questions like this a hundred times on the campaign. *What's the plan? What's your agenda?* I could rattle off a list of policy ideas off the cuff. But that's not what immediately came into my mind.

"I want this government to feel different," I said. "I want people to feel that it's open, that it's listening, and that it's going to bring kindness back."

Kindness. That was the word. It is a child's word, in a way. Simple. And yet it encompassed everything that had ever mattered to me: My father in his uniform in Murupara, agreeing not to arrest a man quite yet, not in a town square, so that the man might preserve a bit of dignity. Hamish's wife taking care of my mother when she fell apart, then my mother taking care of absolutely everyone. All the people I'd known through the years: family and friends, people I'd worshipped alongside or worked with, even fought with, but always—always—in the service of something better.

Some people thought kindness was sentimental, soft. A bit naive, even. I knew this. But I also knew they were wrong. Kindness has a power and strength that almost nothing else on this planet has. I'd seen kindness do extraordinary things—I'd seen it give people hope, I'd seen it change minds and transform lives. I wasn't afraid to say it aloud, and as soon as I did it, I was sure: kindness. This would be my guiding principle, no matter what lay ahead.

"Where are you now?" John Campbell asked, and I told him I was next to a KFC. We laughed, and we talked a little more, about what might change in the days ahead, and how much. And by then I was almost at Government House, and everything was about to begin.

PART THREE

13

What If You Are Not Alone

WITHIN THE WEEK, morning sickness set in decisively and consistently.

It was worst when I woke up. Some mornings, just the motion of getting out of bed made my head spin. I'd rush to the toilet, where I'd slump next to the bowl waiting for the nausea to pass, enough at least to get up off the floor. I could function, and importantly, I could concentrate, but the sickness was always there, all day long.

It was there when our cabinet met for the first time, just hours after my swearing in, and it was there in the days ahead as we hired staff and reviewed the many parts of our one-hundred-day agenda: an ambitious plan, with almost twenty different points of action, some of which required drafting or implementing new laws and others, like our plan to make the first year of university or polytechnic free, which required new systems altogether.

Did I let on that I wasn't feeling well? Of course not. The only people who knew about my pregnancy, still, were Clarke and Julia. Did I let the morning sickness slow me down? Absolutely not. I did what countless women do every day, and what women throughout history have always done—tucked away whatever was going on for me privately and got on with it. I compartmentalized like it was an Olympic sport, held meeting after meeting, stayed focused, and revealed nothing.

And I found small things that helped too: Hot water with lemon. A few water crackers first thing in the morning. And then, blissfully, salt and vinegar potato chips. Piles and piles of them. It was the combination of tang and salt that helped the most, so I began to keep stashes of them in my office, going through one bag after the next.

Thirteen days after my swearing in, not quite three weeks since my life had turned upside down, I awoke in bed with my stomach turning. It was still dark, so I switched on the light on my bedside table, where a sleeve of dry water crackers sat. But I had no time to eat the crackers. Not today. I made it to the bathroom just in time to grab the sides of the porcelain bowl and throw up. Until now, nausea was the thing that plagued me more than vomiting. Now, as I kneeled on the bathroom tiles, I wondered if a cork had been removed.

Clarke stood in the doorframe. "You okay?" In response to his question, I vomited again.

I was not okay. But I had to be. Today was the opening of parliament, the official reconvening of government under its new leadership. *My* new leadership. It would be, as always, a regal affair, full of pomp and ceremony. I moaned, feeling the cool tile floor beneath me. I needed to get up. With the official events just hours away, I flushed the toilet and pulled myself up off the floor. *What if I vomit today, during the state opening? What the hell am I going to do?*

Clarke brought me water and more crackers. I moved slowly. I pulled on tights, a navy-blue dress with an abstract pattern, a black blazer on top. I willed my stomach to settle. I got to the ceremony, and before long the chamber was filled with all 120 MPs and other dignitaries—people in military uniforms, traditional dress, and judicial robes and wigs. And that's when I knew I needed to vomit.

The back of my throat felt constricted, an almost choking feeling. My mouth watered, a sure tell that my stomach couldn't hold even the little that was in it. I mapped my escape route: a door to the right, a bathroom in the "ayes" lobby. But I knew I was being broadcast live, and a prime minister can't just up and leave in the middle of the opening of parliament. *Don't throw up. Don't throw up. Don't throw up.*

Somehow, I managed to hold it together to get through the ceremony, but over the coming weeks, this sort of thing would happen repeatedly. It happened while I was meeting foreign dignitaries at the Beehive. As I chaired meetings of my caucus of MPs. In the middle of press conferences. I felt sick so often that I began to associate the smell of the ninth floor with nausea. Before long, every time I stepped out of the elevator, a wave would hit me.

"The question is, is it okay for the prime minister to take maternity leave while in office?" The words Mark Richardson had asked the morning after I'd become Labour leader kept rolling around in my head as I went over the press statement: PRIME MINISTER ANNOUNCES PREGNANCY.

It was mid-January. My first one hundred days weren't quite up, but we'd still managed by now to make the first year of university or apprenticeships free for students, set up a temporary commission to make policy recommendations on climate change, and passed laws to extend paid leave for parents who needed to take care of their newborns. I was twenty weeks pregnant now. Summer had given me the benefit of loose blouses, but hiding my growing middle was becoming a challenge.

Clarke and I had told our families about my pregnancy during a short summer break, and now it was time to start sharing the news more widely, first with a few staff members, then with Winston Peters, who would take over as prime minister while I was on maternity leave, then with other ministers and MPs, and finally, with the general public. How was this going to land? For three months, I'd been going over that question in my head, getting different answers each time. In my career to date, I thought I'd had a reasonable read on the way people might react to things. On this issue, though, I'd lost all perspective. Some days, I convinced myself that people would be happy for me. Others I was certain that whatever hope I had of being an effective leader would be buried in the commentary of "PM prioritizes family over country."

Part of the announcement was coming up with a post for Instagram. I manage my own social media, and I have so many mixed feelings about the platforms. On the one hand, I like sharing ideas or plans directly, without the filter of commentators. I like the chance to interact and connect with people I'd otherwise never have a chance to meet, to hear people's views, ideas, and even their struggles. But the ease and openness of communicating on the platforms are also part of the reason that spending time on them can be tough, and why sometimes

I knew there were days I just shouldn't go on them. They were places where some people share their own unfiltered feelings—of rage, hatred, bigotry, cruelty—and even where disinformation could spread at incredible speed. And it almost doesn't matter if all of this happens under someone's real name or some anonymous persona they have created—it can feel just as gutting and hurtful to be attacked on social media as it does in real life. So when we got ready for this announcement, the happy news that there would be a baby, I was hoping people would be supportive, but I was also bracing for the worst.

When the day arrived, we rolled out the plan with military precision, which included a press statement that we released at the same time as the announcement on Instagram. We used a simple image. Two fishing hooks sitting side by side. Inside the second was a small hook sitting in its center—a baby hook. Above the words read, *And we thought 2017 was a big year! Clarke and I are really excited that in June . . . I'll be Prime Minister AND a mum, and Clarke will be "first man of fishing" and stay at home dad . . . I know there will be lots of questions, and we'll answer all of them (I can assure you, we have a plan all ready to go!) But for now, bring on 2018.*

I hit post and then waited.

One baby blanket was cheerfully imperfect: bright blocks of color, twenty-four squares in all, each crafted with simple, uneven purl stitches. The blanket had been made by children: reds and yellows, blues and teals, purples and ivories, a single black patch more rectangular than square, attached with seams of yellow into a gloriously lopsided whole. Looking at it, I could imagine the small hands still learning to master their needles and could almost hear the adult voice leading them. *The prime minister is having a baby. Shall our class make a gift for her family?*

The response to the announcement about my pregnancy was almost overwhelming. It began with emails, so many emails. In the twenty-four hours after the news broke, the person who managed correspondence for me—Dinah, who was accustomed to receiving tens of thousands of messages a year—said she'd never seen such an influx.

Before long, a woman named Heather McCracken started a hashtag, #KnitForJacinda, calling on New Zealanders everywhere to craft baby goods and donate them to neonatal units in hospitals. So many people answered the call that before long another New Zealander from the South Island tweeted, "I can't concentrate due to the sound of half of Dunedin knitting booties."

Handmade gifts arrived at the office too. The correspondence team created a display table, and within days it overflowed. I had prepared myself for blowback. I was a public figure, used to judgment and scrutiny. Now I was pregnant *and* unwed. I was also new to the job. If people wanted to make comments about me, they had plenty of reason to. But I hadn't considered a fundamental truth: that politicians are humans first, and perhaps the public hadn't lost sight of that. And so maybe in the beautiful country of New Zealand, the happy news of a baby could be just that: happy.

But for all this support, my pregnancy added a new kind of pressure. I was only the second world leader in history to have a baby in office. The first was Benazir Bhutto. She was the first female to lead Pakistan, and in 1990, two years into her time in office, she had a baby girl. I didn't think the *world's* eyes were on me, but I did think naysayers' were. Those who might be waiting to say: *See, you can't do a demanding job like that and be a mother.* Somehow I had to prove you could do both, and not just for myself, but for any girl who might be watching.

I remembered the many times I'd gone on school visits as an MP and asked the students about their dream jobs. All around the country, boys and girls had equally high aspirations, but when I'd follow up and ask them what job they thought they would actually do, a clear split often emerged. Many of the girls would immediately dial down their goals while the boys couldn't even understand why I was asking the question;

it didn't occur to them that they'd fall short of their dreams. I cannot tell you when it began, but I saw among these girls an undercurrent of self-doubt—one that encouraged them to scale back and self-exclude so early in life. I knew that. I had felt it too. But now I had to prove that it was wrong.

I treated my pregnancy like a test, a set of hurdles to get through without breaking a sweat. There was the pilgrimage to Waitangi in February—not just an important national holiday that marks the signing of the Treaty of Waitangi, but also a major political event, one that was sometimes complicated; it has often been the site of debate and protest by Māori over breaches to the Treaty of Waitangi. But it was also a place of community and whānau, family, and an opportunity for conversation, community building, and importantly, government accountability. Prime ministers typically attended Waitangi for a day and then hosted a small breakfast at a local hotel the next morning. But I wanted our government's relationship with Māori to be different than under previous governments. So instead of going for only one day, we went for five.

We created Te Arawhiti, "the bridge," a new agency to improve the ongoing relationship between government and indigenous New Zealanders. I wanted to affirm that New Zealand's future was tied to the success of all of our communities, and that meant working alongside Māori, who had long endured the legacy of colonization. We held discussions with Māori leaders about improving health care outcomes, increasing employment, and strengthening education. I delivered part of my speech in te reo Māori, the Māori language. Even though I began almost every speech I gave in te reo Māori, here felt different. This was the place the treaty was signed. I knew that as someone who never formally learned te reo Māori, I would stumble, that I would make errors. But I also knew language signaled a commitment to understanding and to bridging gaps.

I finished the trip not with a small invite-only breakfast as had been the practice in the past, but with government ministers behind a BBQ, cooking eggs and bacon for a thousand people. I stood there as the golden sun came up, apron tied over my baby bump, flipping slices of bacon, feeling so optimistic.

On trips like that one, the media were with us around the clock. They were on the ground with me, at every event, meeting, and public meal. I figured, if they were going to be with me, I had to prove I had stamina.

The air was sweltering throughout a tour in March of neighboring Pacific countries, and at one press conference I could see streaks of sweat trickling down journalists' faces. I was dressed modestly, my arms and knees covered, and before long, my feet began to swell, and my shoes, which normally fit comfortably, dug into my skin painfully. But rather than wrap things up, I kept going until there were no more questions and only silence from the gathered press gang, long after the time available had passed. Only then, when I was certain I hadn't been the first one to cave, did I hobble away to shove my feet into a cold bath.

Another work trip in those early months brought me to Buckingham Palace in London, where I had a private meeting with our head of state, Queen Elizabeth. She had, of course, raised her children in the public eye, and I asked if she had any advice for how to handle my child's imminent arrival. Her words sounded so matter of fact, just as Grandma Margaret might have said.

"You just get on with it," she said simply.

Of course you do.

Back at home, we wasted no time implementing a policy agenda we had designed to feel *right*. Six months into our administration, we'd canceled the former government's planned tax cuts and replaced them with measures to help low- and middle-income families. We'd increased the family tax credit, which provided families with newborns $60 each week for their babies' first year, introduced a winter energy payment to help New Zealanders with low incomes to pay their heating bills, and boosted the minimum wage. We introduced plans to reduce carbon emissions and combat climate change, and increased efforts to switch to renewable energy. Now we were examining the way our welfare system was working for people going through tough times.

We *had* a safety net—if you were unemployed, unable to work because of sickness or disability, or a sole parent needing to care for a child, our welfare system was meant to be there for you. But this support wasn't always reaching the people who needed it the most, and the process for accessing it could be unfriendly and alienating, making people in need feel isolated and alone. As an MP, I had visited Work and Income welfare offices many times. I'd met constituents who had stepped through those doors in the most desperate time in their lives, only to be dismissed and told to "call and make an appointment." I'd seen others who'd sat in waiting areas with their child for hours on end, and for all that waiting, they had no guarantee of help.

The difference between what we are and what we could be is the greatest waste. I still often thought about this debate topic from my high school years. What if the difference, that loss of human potential, stemmed not just from big, memorable life events and traumas, but also an endless number of small ones that added up? What if tiny moments of dehumanization accumulate over time, ultimately becoming much more than the sum of their parts? And if so, what if we could do something about that? So our team began rolling out child-friendly spaces. Signs in multiple languages. Improved privacy. Accessible bathrooms. New staff processes that emphasized dignity and a sense of safety.

We were making strong headway on our goals, but I woke each day not knowing what new issue would land on my desk. In one very ordinary week, the unexpected issues included a forestry policy dispute between our partners in our governing coalition; an exotic mosquito and carrier of Japanese encephalitis, a brain disease, found in Kaipara; a fisherman who'd netted five dolphins we'd been working hard to protect, causing a very public ruckus; and a ceremony for a new dining hall in Murupara I was meant to open, which led to a dispute between Māori tribes in the area. Then there was the problem of *M. bovis*, a cattle disease that threatened to wipe out New Zealand's dairy industry, a major employer in a country with more cows than people.

By now I was just several days from my due date. I learned that whenever I traveled to farther-flung locations, local midwives were put on alert. A week later, I did indeed head to the hospital. As we arrived, I texted Winston Peters, who would be taking over in my absence: **Just off to hospital so it's over to you! Speak soon.**

Hours of labor later, on June 21, 2018, our daughter, Neve Te Aroha Ardern Gayford was born. Her middle name, Te Aroha, was the mountain beneath which both of my parents were born, the one that in Māori means simply *the love.*

After six weeks, my maternity leave ended and it was time to return to Wellington, to the Beehive, and to the role of prime minister.

We had a new routine. Most weeks, Clarke, Neve, and I flew back and forth between Premier House in Wellington, the official residence of the prime minister, and our private home in Auckland. While in Wellington, Clarke looked after Neve, strolling her over to the Beehive—a ten-minute walk in good weather—several times a day so I could breastfeed at my desk or in the kitchen next to my office. When Clarke needed to be away for filming, Mum would come and stay, or sometimes Clarke's mum. We were making it work, even if some days, Clarke and I spoke only of breastfeeding schedules and coordinating our calendars.

In September, I was due to speak at the United Nations General Assembly. Since a trip from New Zealand to New York City is too long for a breastfeeding mum to make alone, Clarke, Neve, and I traveled there together. At one event, we three sat down together in New Zealand's designated seating on the General Assembly floor, my eyes moving between Neve and the other speakers. That's when I heard *click, click, click*. I strained around awkwardly. I couldn't see where the noise was coming from until one of my colleagues pointed up to a row of booths above the floor. "There's a few media up there," he said.

Still not really registering that it was us they were interested in, I made stupid faces at Neve while Clarke held her. By the end of the day, these images would travel around the world.

These pictures mark the first time a baby was brought to the floor of the UN General Assembly. But when I look at them—at Neve's double chin, her cheeks bulging around the pacifier in her mouth, her blue-and-white striped dress, a hand-me-down from Louise that Neve would outgrow within weeks—it's not the historic occasion I think about.

Instead, I think about all the people just *outside* of the camera frame: the foreign policy advisor who babysat so we could attend an event with the American president. Our ambassador to the UN, who found bassinets, bottle sterilizers, and Jolly Jumpers to convert his home to a playpen. Clarke, who changed diapers, rocked Neve to sleep, and followed me around for feeds.

I worried that this photo could become a banner for a "woman doing it all" or some kind of proof point that women should never complain about how much they have on their plate because look, here's a woman running a country *and* being a mother. Sure, women *can* do it all—they are mothers, workers, caregivers, change makers, advocates, counselors, cheerleaders, often doing these things with little support. But that doesn't mean they should have to.

Women shouldn't *have* to choose—the way our mothers so often did—between whether they are good at their profession, or a good mother or daughter. There should be support networks, a village, whatever you want to call it, that can help them be all of those things without completely losing themselves in the process. That's what I was blessed to have, at the UN and elsewhere: the love and support of others. And today that's exactly what I say when anyone brings up that photo in the UN, or when they stop me in the supermarket to ask how I did it.

14

What If You Could Show You Care

ON FRIDAY, MARCH 15, 2019, a year and a half into my first term as prime minister, I was in a van heading from one event to another when Kelly Spring, one of the members of my press team, leaned forward.

"Prime Minister," she said. Her voice, which was normally warm and reassuring, was uncharacteristically urgent as she handed me her phone.

"There's been a shooting in Christchurch."

It took several hours to piece together the horror of what had happened. We had so few shootings in New Zealand, and when we did, they were often gang related. This was different. A man had gone on a shooting rampage at two mosques where people were peacefully worshipping during Friday prayers, first at the

Al Noor Mosque and then just minutes later at the Linwood Islamic Centre. He was Australian but chose us because he knew that New Zealand openly welcomed people of all faiths. He wanted to destroy that. He wanted us to turn against one another. So he came to New Zealand, and he attacked our Muslim community. Ultimately, we would learn that he killed fifty-one people and that dozens of others were injured.

Even before I had all the facts, I knew I was going to have to talk about the shooting to the country—I was going to have to share information and make sure people felt calm and safe, when this attacker's plan was to make everyone feel scared and fearful. I had to focus. To map out a plan. I called Grant.

My stomach felt like a ball of fire. I swore. I ranted. I was talking to Grant, asking his advice on what I should say, but in my mind, I was replying to the shooter. "How dare he," I said. I said these words again and again: *How dare he*. How dare this man target our country. How dare he try to turn New Zealanders against one another. How dare he use us in this way.

"An outsider came in and attacked *our* people," I continued. "Some of them might have been born somewhere else, but this was *our* community. They are New Zealanders. They are *us*."

"Jacinda," Grant said. "Just say that."

Later that night, back in my office in Wellington, hours after I made my statement at a somber press conference, I picked up my phone and dialed the number for Gamal Fouda, the imam at Al Noor Mosque, where most of the deaths had occurred.

The light had long faded outside my office window. And even as the phone was ringing, I had no idea what I would say. Here was a man I had never met, who only a few hours earlier had stood at the front of his place of worship while his worshippers, his community, were shot in front of him. I was told that he was in shock.

"Hello," Gamal answered. His voice was so quiet. Behind him I heard more voices, the sounds of a busy hospital.

"Hello, Imam," I said. "This is Jacinda Ardern."

Gamal said nothing in response.

"Imam, can you hear me?"

On the other end of the line, I heard a tiny sound, the smallest possible recognition that he was there, that he heard me. I pictured him standing amid the chaos and despair, desperate families all around him. I thought about all he had seen, all that he could never unsee.

"I am sorry," I told him. "I am so sorry."

Again, he responded only with another small noise. So, I said it again, and yet one more time. I said it until I felt sure he'd heard me.

"I am sorry. I am so, so sorry."

The next morning, I was in my ninth-floor office early, reading over my notes for another press conference, the final before I would head to Christchurch. Leaders of other countries had reached out since the attack. When the American president Donald Trump called, he asked me a couple of questions. We discussed what might happen to the terrorist. I used that word, *terrorist*, specifically, and President Trump asked if we were calling the gunman that.

The man who had done this left a rambling seventy-four-page written statement, a manifesto, full of hatred. He'd decorated his guns with the names of white supremacists who'd also killed Muslims. His intent had been not to just take lives, but also to create fear and to intimidate. But more than that, he'd hoped that his actions might inspire new waves of violence. If that wasn't terrorism, then nothing was. "Yes," I told the president. "This was a white man from Australia who deliberately targeted our Muslim community. He is a terrorist."

Trump did not respond to that. He simply asked if there was anything America could do. I waited just a moment, thought briefly about what a small country like mine might ask of a country as well resourced as the United States. My answer was simple.

"You can show sympathy and love for all Muslim communities."

The streets of Christchurch were decorated with flowers, great bursts of color, along with cards and handmade signs, all left by New Zealanders whose hearts had been broken by this violence. In the car, I stared out at this sea of gifts, these symbols of grief. I could imagine the faces of people who had left them there. I had seen so many of them on the news. Wiping their eyes as they laid bunches of carnations and roses wrapped in cellophane with messages propped up so others could read them and know: No one was alone in their sadness.

I was on my way to the Phillipstown community center where leaders from the local Muslim community had gathered. I had no idea what to expect. But whatever it was, I thought—anger, grief—I would absorb it.

We traveled in a convoy: me, local MPs, ministers responsible for the police and ethnic communities, and leaders from other parties. I'd borrowed a black scarf with gold edging from Julia, and stepping out of the car, I wrapped it over my head, covering my hair in accordance with Muslim custom for women. I was escorted inside, where community members sat waiting on plastic chairs in a small, converted classroom. I recognized immediately the imam from the Linwood Islamic Centre, Lateef Zikrullah Alabi. Just that morning, his image had been on the front page of *The Press*.

Imam Lateef was the first to rise. He clasped his hands

in front of him, wringing them slowly. Outside the window, I could see a photographer moving about, aiming their camera at us, trying to get a decent image through the glass. Then Imam Lateef lifted his head and began to speak. His words were hushed and gentle—and completely unexpected.

Of all the things he could have said in that moment, he thanked us. *He thanked us.* Even as I heard the words, I found them hard to comprehend. He thanked us for being there. He thanked New Zealand and New Zealanders for their support. He thanked the country for sharing in his community's grief. The attack was fueled by hatred, but he spoke about the outpouring of love.

As I listened, and then stood to respond, one of the photographers took a photograph through the window—one that, within a few hours, would be shared widely. In it, my hands are clasped, eyes fixed straight ahead, Julia's dark scarf wrapped around my head. But because the photo was taken from the other side of glass, it captured not only me, but also the reflections of flowers, as well as trees and dapples of sunlight. Darkness and light, all mixed together into a hazy collage.

This photograph, taken by Kirk Hargreaves, would be called a "defining image" of my leadership, "an image of hope," "the face of empathy." But all these comments felt backward to me, like an inversion of reality. Even now, when I see this picture, when I think of the moments before the camera recorded this image, I do not see myself. I see a good and gentle soul who'd been broken by horror, and somehow still managed to lead with his heart. The image was a lesson in leadership, that's true. But it was Imam Lateef, not me, who gave it.

My second meeting was at Hagley College, where a crisis center had been established for victims and their loved ones. So many people were still desperately waiting for information. Late the previous night, my chief press secretary, Andrew Campbell, had received a call from a distressed man whose brother was among the missing. He needed to know: Was his brother dead? And if so, why couldn't his body be returned so the family could give him his final passage?

The Muslim faith calls for the bathing, shrouding, and burial of the deceased as quickly as possible—and at most within twenty-four hours. By the time we arrived at the crisis center, more than twenty hours had passed. But the mosques were crime scenes; police and forensic teams were still gathering evidence. That meant all the victims were still lying at the mosques.

Even when that process was done, it would give way to another: The deceased would be transported to emergency morgues that had been established at the Christchurch hospital so they could be officially identified. Since this was what the coroners call a mass fatality incident, the identification process would take time. In other words, not only were we unsure when the bodies would be returned, there was still no definitive list of those who had been killed.

Within the government, we were grappling with state procedures and religious expectations, trying to meet both, but at this point only one thing was clear: The bodies wouldn't be released anytime soon.

But no one had told that to the families yet. I knew that I would have to.

As we arrived at the building where families had gathered, the cool morning air had given way to a warm day. Around the perimeter of the college hall, gang members in leather jackets had been standing guard. They had no formal connection to the Muslim community; rather, they were self-appointed protection from any white supremacists who might be tempted to harass or further terrorize grieving families. I adjusted my headscarf and stepped into the building. In the hallway, a handful of Red Cross workers sat at a table. I couldn't yet see into the main hall, but I could already feel the heat of those inside.

The room was packed. Hundreds of people crammed together, all straining to hear a man at the front of the room who spoke into a microphone. Half the people were responding to what he was saying, while others were begging those around them to be quiet so they could hear. The room felt full of pent-up fear and frustration.

I made my way through the throng of people to Gamal, the imam from Al Noor who had struggled to speak during our call the previous night. He greeted me gently, with words I could not hear above the noise. His eyes were ringed with dark circles.

In the room, there was no stage, no podium or elevated platform, no natural place from which to address the crowd. If I spoke into the microphone, it would only add to the noise. So instead, I extended my arms, pressing them downward, a gesture that invited people to sit. For a few long beats, this is all I did.

People began to sit, a few at a time. One row, then another. Before long, the room was still and quiet. People waited. Some held up phones, connecting me to loved ones, many listening from the other side of the world.

I took a breath. "As-salamu alaykum." *Peace be with you.* The shakiness of my voice surprised me. But I kept going. After speaking for several minutes, sharing in their grief as best I could, questions came from the floor, including about the return of loved ones.

I took in a breath, answered slowly and clearly, and told them the truth: The bodies were still at the mosques. We knew how important it was that they be removed and reunited, and everyone was working as quickly as they could. But identification would take time. We would work efficiently and hard, and we would take religious custom seriously. But there was no denying it would take time. I wasn't sure what response I would get, but as I said the words, I felt sure that it was the right thing to do.

In front of me, one man began to nod, and then there was a calm stillness in the room. Perhaps even bad news can be better than unanswered questions.

That evening, after we called on our counterparts in the Australian government to lend us additional personnel for the victim identification process, the police released a provisional list of the deceased. For the families of the victims, we had confirmed the worst.

As I left the crisis center, I met a woman whose husband was missing. They were tourists, on holiday from Fiji. He'd gone to the mosque for Friday prayers. She hadn't heard from him since, and she didn't know if he was alive. Strangers had driven her around the city, helping her contact hospitals. Now, with no information, they'd brought her here, hoping that someone could finally help her. The woman looked exhausted, dwarfed by the crowd around her. But she also looked determined and utterly focused.

I took her by the arm and led her to a Red Cross disaster relief worker. "I can help from here," the worker said. I hesitated to leave her, but I knew my job wasn't to fix the individual issues in front of me; I had to understand what we needed to do as a government. *The Red Cross will help her,* I told myself, before eventually leaving for the hospital.

My first hospital visit was to the intensive care unit, but there would be many more in the days and weeks and months ahead. I would move from room to room, talking to families, taking in stories. I met a man who'd been shot in the leg and whose five-year-old daughter now lay unconscious in a small child's bed. He couldn't stop retracing his steps, second guessing all the decisions he'd made, searching for some scenario in which his child would have been safe. I met Syrian refugees who came to New Zealand to escape the civil war in their home country, only to lose both a father and son. A second son had survived but was also shot. I met a man who ran a food outlet who'd been shot in the shoulder and didn't know when he could return to work, if he could ever return.

On every visit, at every bedside, I was shaken not only by how many people were injured, but by how many injuries they had. Almost no one had just one injury, a single gunshot wound. They had multiple. The terrorist had used several firearms, including an AR-15, capable of shooting sixty rounds per minute, and the violence caused by this weapon was almost incomprehensible.

That night, I returned to the Defence Force airfield at the Christchurch airport in order to return to Wellington. The space was vast and impersonal: an industrial hangar with metal ceilings and concrete floors, surrounded by chain link. I sat down in a hard plastic chair, and for the first time all day, I fell apart.

I was completely out in the open, on full display, with a handful of the entourage and staff that had accompanied me all day, as well as air force personnel, and yet it was the most private moment I'd had all day. I'd been surrounded by so much grief, and somehow it had helped keep my own in check. My job had been to hold myself together: to focus on other people's grief, not mine. Now, on a plastic chair in the middle of an airport hangar, my own came flooding out.

One of the MPs from the delegation approached with a Styrofoam cup of tea. Wordlessly he handed me the cup, then patted my shoulder. Then Andrew, my press secretary, approached. He must not have seen my face at first, because he immediately began talking about my upcoming interviews.

"You have two live crosses. We'll start with TV One . . ." The moment he really looked at me, his face changed. I could only imagine how I must have appeared. Swollen red eyes, blotchy face, streaks of mascara running down my cheeks.

"Um . . . Your first interview is in five minutes," he said. Then he gestured toward my face a little vaguely. "Can you do something about . . . that?" He was right. I needed to do something about that. There was so much more to be done: more briefings, more interviews, more announcements and updates and statements.

The terrorist had appeared in court that morning. There was the issue of the bodies. And there were other things I was determined the government would do: Replace income for victims who could no longer work and for the families who'd lost their primary earner. Cover the cost of burials. Help ensure that victims and family members who'd had temporary visas could have permanent residency. I knew it was okay to grieve, to feel sad and overwhelmed, but right then was neither the time nor the place. I pulled myself together, thinking, *I can't let myself do that again.*

Five days after the shooting, I visited Cashmere High School in Christchurch, where two of the younger victims had attended school. As I entered, hundreds of students greeted me in the gymnasium by performing the haka, the only act I have ever known to evoke, all at once, power, pride, and grief.

When it was time to speak, I pulled out a small piece of paper with a few notes. I told the students we must remember the people we lost, not the person who took their lives. I told them it was okay to feel sad, and that while it might be hard to express emotions, it was okay to ask for help.

As I finished, I asked the students if they wanted to ask me anything. For a few beats, there was only silence. Then a small girl near the front row raised her hand. Slowly, with thoughtful deliberation, she asked a question I didn't expect: "How are you?"

"How am I?" I repeated her words.

Someone had called me "New Zealand's chief mourner." At the time I hadn't been sure how I felt about this. *Was* I the chief mourner? And was that a good thing? I'd been trying to focus on the grief of those who'd been most affected. But a journalist had recently asked me if I cried at night when I went home. *Of course* I cried at home. On the very first night I returned to Premier House, long after Neve had gone to sleep, I'd found Clarke waiting for me at the end of the hall, and I'd cried into his shoulder for what felt like an eternity. But I wasn't going to tell that to a reporter. How would sharing that moment have helped anyone?

And yet here was this girl, asking me directly how I was. Just moments ago, I'd told the students—all of whom had just lost two schoolmates to unthinkable violence—that it was okay to grieve. *How was I?* I tried to keep my voice from breaking as I managed to say three words, the shortest possible sentence, but also the only words that could convey how I felt. "I'm very sad."

After the questions ended, and the students performed again, the girl made her way to the front of the room. Now that she was standing, I could clearly see her wide eyes, her blond hair hung down her back. She was quite possibly among the youngest in the room, and yet she had the courage and the wisdom to know that age and power don't determine who needs comfort, and who can be a comforter.

Maybe that's why she approached me, and without saying a word, she hugged me.

15

What If You Could Answer the Call for Change

THERE WOULD BE a number of events to mark what happened on March 15, but two especially stand out in my memory. The first was exactly one week after the terrorist attack, as the Muslim community returned to their Friday prayers. We asked the national radio station to play the Arabic call to prayer. Simultaneously, the city of Christchurch converted the largest park in the city, Hagley Park, just steps from Al Noor Mosque, into an outdoor prayer space.

Inside the mosque, there were still bullet holes in walls. By now, all the victims had been identified, and the last of the bodies had finally been released to their families. The streets of Christchurch were covered with personal messages and memorials, sunflowers and lilies and gerbera daisies and hydrangeas, so many flowers they obscured entire pavements. There were candles too, and teddy bears, and so many hand-painted signs: WE ARE ONE, and LET LOVE SHINE, and YOU ARE LOVED.

Thousands of people streamed into the park—fifteen thousand by some estimates, all there to show solidarity with the worshippers. The scene was a defiant rejection of hate, of whatever it was the terrorist had hoped to accomplish. I knew similar gatherings were occurring in Auckland and Wellington, and all around the world. At the exact time of the shooting, the call to prayer rang out around the country, and then, silence.

I scanned the crowd. I willed for calm, peace, no disruption. Gamal appeared on the stage and took the microphone. Speaking with the same gentle softness I'd heard six days before, he said that his community was brokenhearted, but not broken. As he finished, I stood at a mic positioned nearby offering a quote from the Prophet Muhammad, describing New Zealand's grief. "When any part of the body suffers, the whole body feels pain."

As I took my seat, I noticed a young Muslim man standing at the edge of the worship area. His frame was small, his shoulders hunched. He was calling for his mother, his eyes searching the crowd. I watched as he moved toward the microphone, grabbed it, and began to speak. But by this point, the service had started, and the microphone had been cut off. Whatever he was saying went unheard.

He was near me now, and as he turned away from the microphone, his eyes locked onto mine. "Jacinda Ardern," he said, as if he was surprised to see me there. I recognized him: It was the young man who'd lost his brother, the one who called Andrew's cell phone the night of the attack, desperate to find his loved one. He stood there, eyes on mine, and he repeated my name again and again.

Members of the community saw him, standing alone. They took him round the shoulders, gently leading him away—and then he was gone. I'd seen a lot of pain, especially in that last week. But sitting there in that open park, the sun beating down overhead, watching this young man struggling to make sense of a loss that made no sense whatsoever, was then, and remains today, the surest image of grief I've ever seen.

The second event that is indelible in my memory was the National Day of Remembrance: Ko Tātou, Tātou—We Are One, where more than twenty thousand New Zealanders gathered two weeks after the shooting. At this event, I was met by a kuia, a respected matriarch from the local tribe, who hung a kākahu, a ceremonial cloak, around my shoulders as the karanga began.

A karanga is like no other sound I know. Made by Māori women, it joins the living to the spiritual world. It is deep and guttural, both a song and a lament. I have heard the karanga countless times, and every time it moves me. But as it rang out across the open park and settled on the thousands of people who had gathered, it felt like a blanket enveloping a group of strangers together.

Not long after the karanga—after the names of every one of the fifty-one victims was read aloud, after a man whose wife had died in the attack spoke, incredibly, about forgiveness—someone I'd never seen before stepped onto the stage. He was in his early seventies, with a trimmed white beard and sunglasses. He was dressed simply in black slacks and a black polo, with a small piece of pounamu, a treasured form of jade stone, around his neck. With only his acoustic guitar and an upright bass as accompaniment, he began strumming a tune so familiar it felt almost like it was coming from inside of me. Then he sang:

"I've been smilin' lately
Dreaming about the world as one"

The singer was Yusuf Islam, the man once known as Cat Stevens, and the song, "Peace Train," was the one I had first heard thirty years before, as I sat on the floor in middle school. Tears had streamed down my face that day; they did now too.

The weapons used in the March 15 terrorist attack involved six firearms, including two AR-15-style rifles, a semiautomatic, and a pump-action shotgun. The terrorist had acquired them all legally, and then modified them to make them even more destructive.

The terrorist wasn't a citizen. He was a newcomer to New Zealand, having arrived just eighteen months prior. And yet we had given him a license to use weapons that had been designed with a single purpose: to kill as many people as possible in as short a time as possible.

There is no constitutional right to own a gun in New Zealand. But gun ownership isn't rare. Up and down New Zealand, people learn to use weapons to shoot deer or target goats and other pests. When I was younger, I had learned to shoot a gun to deal with possums on our orchard.

Through the years, there had been some attempts to change our gun laws, but most hadn't gone far. Now the unthinkable had happened. I was determined: Our gun laws would change. Within three days of the shooting, the cabinet agreed in principle to move forward with reform.

But reform isn't a general thing. It requires committing to specifics: specific definitions, standards, and procedures. Sometimes these required making judgment calls. Our focus was on high-capacity weapons, but what counted as "high" capacity, exactly? Duck hunters often used pump-action shotguns. These are also one of the most common weapons found on farms to manage pests. Some pump-action shotguns had a five-round capacity. Others, a ten-round. How many did a hunter or farmer need? We went back and forth on this question, debating the line between meaningful reform and unnecessary burden.

Five days after the March 15 attack, I was finishing up a meeting with first responders at a police station in Christchurch when an idea occurred to me. "I have a quick question," I said. "How many of you hunt?" Nearly every hand went up.

"And I'm guessing many of you use pump-action shotguns?"

Most nodded. They did.

"So perhaps you can help me," I said. "If you're a hunter, or a farmer, what's a reasonable number of rounds for a pump-action shotgun? If *you* were rewriting the law, where would the cutoff be?"

There was no one better prepared to reflect on the question than this group of people. They used weapons, and they faced weapons. They were recreational hunters and professional first responders to situations that involved armed criminals.

Almost instantly, their silence transformed into a lively discussion. They talked through the options and came to consensus.

"Five rounds," one said, as the others nodded along. "You don't need ten for a hunt. Five will do."

I thanked them. The moment may have been impromptu,

but this group was the most informed, thoughtful focus group I could possibly have assembled, and I was grateful. When I got into the car, I called my legislative team. "I think we have an answer to our shotgun issue."

Seventeen days after the shooting, we put the new law before parliament. Ten days after that, the law passed with the support of all but one member of parliament. The law created an amnesty and buyback program, which allowed people who owned the weapons we'd just made illegal to be compensated for turning in their guns.

In the first month after the law passed, ten thousand weapons were handed in to the police. These were simple transactions. We created collection points. People brought their banned guns. In exchange, they were handed cash. Then they went home.

By the year's end, fifty-six thousand weapons and nearly two hundred thousand gun parts would be handed in and destroyed.

More sensible gun reforms would still be needed, but we wouldn't win every battle. A gun registration program we tried later—allowing officials to know how many guns, and of what type, were held by gun owners, which also allowed medical professionals to know if a patient was at risk from weapons at home—would also pass, but with less unanimity, putting the policy at risk of being undone by future parliaments.

But we'd acted. We'd done *something.* And just as important, we'd proved that something can be done.

Today, when I speak to groups of people abroad, there is one line that invariably draws spontaneous applause: *We reformed our gun laws in ten days.* The applause isn't a once-in-a-while thing. It happens literally every time I say those words. That response tells me that even in countries where gun violence feels intractable, and reform near impossible, people haven't given up. They refuse to accept violent extremism as inevitable and gun violence as some kind of new normal.

But it also tells me something else: That every crisis asks clearly and unequivocally for action to be taken. And it will keep asking. Until there is change.

There was also the issue of the video. The shooter had live streamed the attack—a full seventeen minutes of it—before it was stopped. For the first twenty-four hours afterward, the video was shared at a rate of once per second on YouTube, and Facebook removed 1.5 million copies of it.

I even stumbled on the video myself, soon after the attack, when I'd opened Instagram to post information for the public. I was heading to the airport, and the video's presence in my feed had been so shocking, so viscerally horrible, I'd thrown my phone down onto the floor of the van.

If I had seen it, how many others had? How many still would? And what impact would that have?

Not only was this video created to revictimize those who were harmed and their families, it was intended to become a weapon itself—to encourage both copycats and revenge attacks. I would hear repeated stories of people who had seen it: family members, friends, members of the Muslim community. I couldn't imagine a world where the worst possible thing had happened to you—the murder of a loved one—only for it to be recorded for the world to see.

In the days after the attack, social media companies like Facebook reached out and asked to meet. But I knew if I met with them, there would likely be an apology, maybe a photo op, and then they would be gone. There was a chance that nothing would change. For a brief moment in time, we had an opportunity to ask for more.

I called leaders from around the world and asked them if they would join New Zealand to build a bigger ask. When they agreed, I called Mark Zuckerberg of Facebook. I called Jack Dorsey, who ran Twitter at the time, and Sundar Pichai at Google, then YouTube's CEO, Susan Wojcicki, Amazon's Jeff Bezos, and critically, Brad Smith, the president of Microsoft, who became a key supporter of our work. Within eight weeks we constructed and launched what became known as the Christchurch Call to Action, a commitment to eliminate terrorist and violent extremist content online.

As I write, governments, civil society, and major companies—more than 130 of them in all—have joined the Christchurch Call. Because of this, there are new crisis protocols, tools, and policies that exist today that didn't before the attacks on March 15. These range from a global crisis response system to stop the spread of live-streamed attacks, controls on live streaming established by tech platforms, and investment in new tools to help researchers understand the influence of algorithms and how people are radicalized online.

Violence inspires more violence. And so long as that cycle continues online, and offline, the work to resist violence must go on.

Years have passed since March 15. But I still think all the time about those days after the attacks.

I remember Imam Lateef's gentle strength, Gamal's thoughtful courage, the grief and kindness that overflowed from a devastated nation. I think about the meeting at the crisis center, the way it felt to share difficult news, and all those terrible and beautiful moments in the hospital—the strength and love and goodness I witnessed again and again and again. I hear the soaring melody of "Peace Train." So much about the world had changed since I first heard that song. I too had changed. I had seen more and begun to understand just how cruel and dark the world could be. Yet sitting there, I was just as committed to a world in which we took care of one another.

And I still believe that when faced with a choice between hatred and hope, you must choose hope every time. For all that though, the sadness of March 15 has never left me. But perhaps some sadness is never meant to, because that's what keeps you focused on change.

16

What If You Could Do Things Differently

A FEW YEARS before I was elected prime minister, I had been campaigning for Grant to become the leader of the Labour Party when questions came up about his sexuality. Some media speculated publicly: *Is New Zealand ready for a gay leader?* I knew Grant was concerned about the impact the discussion over his sexuality might have. "I worry," Grant told me privately, "about the young people watching." This was a common refrain from him. After all, he had once been one of those young people.

It was around this time that I took part in a fundraiser for a youth LGBTQ+ organization in Auckland. That's when I heard someone call my name. The voice was unfamiliar, but something in its tone told me that this was someone who knew me.

I turned around to see the person standing in front of me

dressed head to toe in a figure-hugging gold dress, large platform shoes, and an enormous beehive hairdo above shimmering eyeshadow and red painted lips. A glamorous and self-assured drag queen. They were gorgeous. But did I know them?

Apparently, I did. "Jacinda, it's *me*," they said. There was something about their stance, the softness of their face. Some deep memory began to unlock. Yes, maybe I did know them.

"It's me," they continued. "It's *Walter*."

In a flash, it was suddenly so obvious. Walter, my sweet Mormon friend from Murupara. The gentle child who'd collected perfume cards all those years ago, who'd played the wolf in our church production of Little Red Riding Hood. Walter, who joined me as we dressed up together as Smurfs for school but was so desperate to be Smurfette that we traded, so I went to school that day as Papa Smurf. *Of course. Walter.* We laughed and hugged, and in those few short moments, it felt as though more than twenty-five years hadn't passed.

There were so many questions I wanted to ask, but time didn't allow. Instead, I left our short meeting that day believing undisputedly that every child should have the opportunity to be their true selves and live up to their potential. Whether you are born into a Mormon household or an agnostic one, a small town like Murupara or a big city like Auckland—we are who we are, and no one should ever be told that is not enough.

Not Grant. Not Walter. Not any child.

Not ever.

Ever since my early days as an MP, I'd *always* focused on children. Back when I was in opposition, I'd specifically asked to lead the children's portfolio, which includes policy for a range of issues that affect the lives of children and families. Now that I was a mum, I also thought almost daily about the strength of parents who raised children on their own, and what support they might need. I felt sure that if we thought more about families' experiences as a whole, we could help our smallest and youngest thrive. And if we focused our policymaking on that, our country as a whole would be better off.

We often claimed that New Zealand was the best place in the world to raise a child. There was truth to this. We had free health care for all kids, a strong education system, and beaches, forests, and rural landscapes that created an incredible "backyard" for a child.

But I also wanted us to be the best place in the world to *be* a child. And we weren't there yet. We didn't have enough affordable housing or mental health services. We had high levels of child poverty and family violence. Fixing these issues wouldn't be simple or quick. But while I knew there would be no miracles, I also knew there could be no change if we kept accepting that the old systems were sufficient.

For years, Grant had promoted the idea of moving beyond simplistic economic measures like GDP—gross domestic product, the gold standard for assessing a nation's success. GDP measures the value of all the goods and services produced in a nation in a given year, everything from farm products to furniture and from the work of barbers to that of bankers. Grant was now our finance minister, the most important job in the cabinet outside of prime minister, and he wanted to capture not only how much money was flowing through our economy, but the wider health and well-being of our nation. *A business owner could be pumping pollution into our waterways*, I'd heard Grant say before, *and struggling with mental health issues within their family. But as long as that business is making a profit and paying taxes, GDP will say all is well.*

By mid-2019, we were finally in the position to construct a budget we wanted, one that moved beyond GDP as the sole measure of our well-being and indicator for where investment should be directed. Under Grant's leadership, we produced something called the Wellbeing Budget. It wasn't just a title; it was a whole new way of thinking about the impact of the budget and the effects of what we would debate in parliament. Initiatives that contributed the most to our national well-being were prioritized with funding. Among other things, this meant we made a four-year $1.9 billion investment in mental health initiatives.

The mental health work always felt personal. It had been more than twenty-five years since I'd learned my friend Fiona's brother had taken his own life, and that incident had never left me. In the years since, I'd met so many people who either had struggled in some way themselves or knew someone who had.

Everyone knew someone. And every story I heard, every mother who told me about losing a child to suicide, every person who'd told me about losing a brother, a parent, an uncle, a friend, always brought me right back to that day, the helpless despair I'd felt when one of the brightest, cleverest kids I'd known suddenly was no longer there.

So much of government work comes down to statistics. Targets. Goals and progress as measured by trend lines on a graph. But with the issue of mental health and suicide, I couldn't see the issue through the lens of numbers. These were human beings: relatives, friends, a best friend's brother. So, when it came time to set targets for our work—benchmarks by which we'd measure how successful our work had been—I struggled.

In our first one hundred days we set up an inquiry into our mental health and addiction services. Our team of experts, including people who had used the mental health system themselves, set a target of 20 percent reduction in suicide rates by 2030. I rejected it.

Officials pressed us. They pointed out that I'd accepted nearly all the other forty recommendations. They said that it would stand out if I didn't accept this too.

But I couldn't. The idea of standing up in front of a grieving family and telling them that so long as there weren't *as many* suicides, we would have met our goal, felt wrong.

"If not twenty percent, then what *is* the target?" an advisor pressed me. "Do we have one?"

I did. I knew this target would be criticized, dismissed as unrealistic, and completely unattainable. It meant guaranteed failure. But any other number would tell the public that we had a tolerance for tragedy and the loss of life. And I didn't.

"The target is zero," I insisted. The health minister agreed, and that is what we announced.

In 2020 we declared Matariki, the Māori New Year, a new public holiday—the first holiday unique to Māori. When we officially marked this lunar event in 2022, it was midwinter, and cold that evening as Clarke, Neve, and I gathered with other families huddled together in coats and scarves under sparkling constellations. I hung back, watching as Clarke hoisted Neve onto his shoulders, just another father and daughter blending in with the crowd in the darkness. There were so many people who had gathered for the Matariki events—for dawn services, school events, and sunset walks. I thought about what this new holiday meant: generations of children who would learn about the full traditions of their birth country in a way that my own never did.

A year before my election as prime minister, parliament was presented with a petition started by two teens, Leah Bell and Waimarama Anderson, students from a public school in New Zealand. They couldn't understand why every young New Zealander didn't learn in school about New Zealand history, including the New Zealand Wars, the series of conflicts between British colonial troops and Māori in the nineteenth century. Bell and Anderson collected thirteen thousand signatures for their petition to create a commemoration of the wars. During the hearing that followed the petition presentation, the girls were asked about the long impact of their efforts. Waimarama answered, "This nation will be a peaceful, honest, united, and conscious country."

That was exactly the sentiment that inspired me, one year into office, to make the teaching of New Zealand history in schools compulsory. When I was a kid, teaching it had been optional, a choice I was lucky Mr. Fountain had made. But now all our young people would learn about our past, to help us better understand our present, even those who didn't happen to have a Mr. Fountain in the front of their classroom. This was, and remains, one of the policies of which I am most proud. It was about more than curriculum; it was about nation building.

Indigenous Māori had generously shared language, cultural practices, and values that made New Zealand unique, from pōwhiri, the act of welcoming newcomers, to manaakitanga—showing kindness, generosity, and care for others. This was a grace that in my mind could only be fully appreciated if we all understood the often-brutal history that had preceded it. In other words, if we could help build people's understanding of our own country, and the rich heritage that each of us has brought to it, perhaps we could repair our cracks along the way.

Over my time in government, our focus on children's issues would see us increase welfare payments for families with children, build more state houses than any government had in the last fifty years, expand access to early childhood education and health care, invest in violence prevention programs, and roll out free sanitary products in schools for young people who had their periods. But making New Zealand the best place to be a child also meant gathering ideas directly from an unexpected source: kids themselves. We consulted with kids about their dreams, desires, and ambitions. And sometimes, they even helped us make policy.

After I entered office, we received a series of petitions from kids from different schools around the country urging us to ban single-use plastics, like disposable shopping bags, because of their harm to the environment, particularly to ocean life. Some students were invited to testify before the Environment Committee, and they noted that by 2050, there will be more plastic in the ocean by weight than there will be fish. These petitions were signed by tens of thousands of New Zealanders and gave our government a sense of just how widespread support for a ban was. So, in August of 2018, we announced a phaseout of single-use plastic bags over the following year.

In June 2019, we launched another program: Child and Youth Wellbeing Strategy. The year prior, we had passed a child poverty reduction law, which set targets to cut child poverty in half over the next ten years. Now we were launching a plan to ensure that every New Zealand child could live in a home where they were safe and loved and had what they needed to thrive.

When we started developing the strategy, we invited children to share what they hoped for. Thousands of postcards went out, and in response, we received drawings, images, and handwritten notes. I read every one when they came in. The team working on the strategy framed some of these postcards, which I hung at the entry to the Premier House apartment so I couldn't go home, or leave for work, without seeing them.

Being with your family.

To be accepted. To be understood and taken seriously.

If the parents are good, then the kids are good.

We decided to do the formal launch of the Child and Youth Wellbeing Strategy, alongside a new program to improve food in schools, at a primary school in Rotorua, the city where my family used to grocery shop back when we lived in Murupara. A range of dignitaries and leaders would join us for the launch. I was proud of the work and excited to share it with them.

When we stepped into the school hall full of several hundred middle school children, the kids burst into an energetic performance of the haka. Their eyes were wide, their voices strong. They slapped their hands on their legs with all their might. In the front row, one of the kids—a boy with a buzz cut, probably no more than ten years old, lean legs poking through his shorts—looked directly at me as he moved. His performance was intense. The kids around him were performing the haka brilliantly. But this boy—he was *feeling* it.

After the speeches were finished, we stepped out from the hall and back into the light of the day. "That performance . . ." I said to a staff member, struggling to find words to describe it. She was already nodding.

"They practiced all week when they heard you were coming," she said, and then gave me a smile as we walked.

The school visit was one of many stops for me that day, but for those kids, and especially that boy, it was everything. He had something to say, something he could best express through the haka, and I felt so honored that I was there to see it. There was nothing small about that.

17

What If Doing Your Best Is Enough

ONE NIGHT, IN early 2022, when Neve was about three and a half, I returned from a long day at the office and peeked in at her. I thought she might be asleep, but from her bed, she whispered, "Mummy?"

"Yes, darling," I said, setting my briefcase down. "It's just me."

Neve sat up in bed, her stuffed animals piled around her. I sat down on the edge of the bed, rubbing her back, hoping I could coax her back to sleep.

Neve rarely complained about my work, and that surprised me. When she'd been born, I feared she would constantly bemoan my absence. But that hadn't happened at all. What I felt—that constant ache that I should be with her more—had been created by me, all on my own. But tonight, Neve finally asked me the question I had been waiting for: "Mummy, why do you have to work so much?"

We had never told Neve I was the prime minister. We hadn't exactly *hidden* the fact of my job, but nor did we explain it. I wanted her to know me as "Mumma" and nothing else. Not long ago, when someone had asked Neve if she knew what her mum did for a living, she'd answered "eat chocolate," a reference to the stash of chocolates in a drawer in my desk that she loved to seek out when she visited me at the Beehive. But now she wasn't asking me *what* I did. She was asking me *why*.

"Well, my darling," I said now, straightening her pajamas over her back and covering her small frame with the duvet. "I have a very important job."

"Like looking after me?"

In the dark, a set of twinkle lights glowed through a jar on her bedside table.

"Yes," I answered her. "Like looking after you. That is my most important job. But I look after other people too."

Neve nodded along earnestly, satisfied with that answer, not realizing that her simple question, *Why do you have to work so much?* had gotten to the heart of my dilemma, and that of parents everywhere. Our children are the most important thing to us, our greatest priority. But the most simplistic measure of that love and care is time. I had done everything to demonstrate my love by every other measure: affection, comfort, patience, my endless striving to be present.

But time kept betraying me.

One Saturday morning, a few months later, Neve asked to play hide-and-seek. In the hallway she started counting to five, fast at first, then more slowly. Her hands only partially covered her face, and as I raced into the lounge, I could see her eyes peeking through her small fingers. I ducked behind an oversize upholstered armchair.

"Here I come!" Neve shouted. She charged into the lounge, pacing theatrically like a miniature bloodhound.

Then she asked, "Now, where is that prime minister?"

Where is that prime minister? I had to hold myself back from popping up from my hiding spot to ask her where she heard that. But I stayed quiet, and before long, her head appeared, giggling over the back of the chair.

"Found you!" she shouted, delighted.

After some quick cheers, I asked, "Neve, what did you call me?" She laughed knowingly. Then, as if happy to keep up a ruse, she shrugged, almost as if the words had never passed her lips. "I don't know, Mumma." Then she was off again. "Your turn!"

Before long it was Neve's fourth birthday, and I was preparing to make her a cake. For her third birthday, Neve had asked Clarke for not one, but *three* different themes: *Moana*, *Frozen*, and Mickey Mouse. The request might have thrown many a parent, but not Clarke. He constructed a cake in the shape of an old tube TV, with licorice antennae, a stand of chocolate fingers, and dials of chopped "licorice logs." He covered the cake in white fondant icing, outlining the "screen" in licorice straps. He then spent hours mounting a projector above the table, from which he projected onto the fondant scenes from *Moana*, *Frozen*, and Mickey Mouse cartoons. The images filled the screen area precisely, and the whole thing was operated by remote control. It was, I admit, incredible: Neve literally "watched" her cake before eating it.

Now it was my turn. I made a red ladybug.

As the months passed, a thought entered my mind and stayed stubbornly stuck there: Maybe it was time for me to go.

In the last five years we'd dealt with so much: a large-scale cattle disease, a domestic terror attack, a volcanic eruption, floods, wildfires, another election, and leading the country through the intense stress and strain of the global COVID-19 pandemic, which had caused illness and death; the closures of borders, businesses, and schools; lockdowns and restrictions on travel; and all the anger these challenges brought. We were now in a period of relative calm; the COVID virus was winding down and we could safely reopen the country, return people to their regular routines. There was a steadiness to the days again. But I couldn't enjoy them, couldn't relax into the relative tranquility.

I'd been running on adrenaline for so long. All those sleepless nights, it wears a person out. My fuse was shorter and I had less patience for all the politicking, less willingness to soften my frustration with a smile. My stress wasn't just something I was feeling on the inside. It seemed to be something I wore on the outside too. People often told me I looked tired. Gaunt. *Maybe you should eat a meat pie*, more than one person had suggested to me. Fair point. When I was stressed, I couldn't eat, and these days, I was always stressed.

I had been conditioned to crisis. I knew the next challenge, whatever it was, lay just around the corner. And when it came, I would need a full tank, more than enough in reserves. And I wasn't sure I had that anymore.

Every day, people demanded I prove myself, and I had. I was finished proving myself. There was only one question I needed to answer now, and it wasn't one that would be posed by my critics. It was my own: *Did I want to keep going?*

One of my favorite things to do as a politician was to visit schools. Even as prime minister I had tried to visit as many schools as possible. On most of my school visits, I'd go through an exercise with students on leadership, asking them the same question: "What does a politician look like?" I did this exercise dozens of times through the years, going back to when I was a newly elected MP. I would ask the students to close their eyes. To tell me what they physically saw, as well as what they heard. The words that would come flying sometimes broke my heart: *Man. Aggressive. Confident. Selfish. Old. Gray. Untrustworthy. Liar. Bald.*

It was never lost on me that there I was, a politician, standing in front of students and asking them to describe one, only to have them describe traits that belonged to someone else. But that was my point. I was trying to explore our underlying assumptions. To show that sometimes we think that jobs or roles require you to have certain traits or ways of being, and maybe that was something we should challenge.

On a school visit near the end of my second term as prime minister, I put my usual question to the young people, maybe fifteen or sixteen years old, sitting on the floor in front of me. "What does a politician look like?"

For the first time, I noticed some differences. The word *woman* was used, for starters. Not all of the traits were those of type A personalities either. I saw a girl in the front slowly, tentatively raise her hand. I gestured to her, and she sat forward a little bit as she offered me a word that in all these years no student ever had.

"Kind," she said. "I think politicians can be kind."

I smiled at her. "Yes," I said. "I think they can be kind too."

Years earlier, I had counted myself out of politics, assuming that a politician who was kind, or who was sensitive, maybe even filled with self-doubt, was one destined to fail. The template for political leadership, it seemed, was too rigid to be broken. And yet here I was now, prime minister, standing in front of a girl who was saying the very thing that once seemed impossible. Maybe that meant it would be different for her.

Maybe by the time this girl was my age, kindness in politics wouldn't be unusual, it would be the norm. Maybe we'll have many, many leaders who don't fit old assumptions. Perhaps that young girl will even be one of them. If she is, she might have doubts along the way, she might question herself, her ability to be there. And if she does, here is what I would say to her. Here is what I would say to everyone who doesn't fit the old mold:

If you have impostor syndrome, or question yourself, channel that. It will help you. You will read more, seek out advice, and humble yourself to situations that require humility to be conquered. If you're anxious and overthink everything, if you can imagine the worst-case scenario always, channel that too. It will mean you are ready when the most challeng-

ing days arrive. And if you are thin-skinned and sensitive, if criticism cuts you in two, that is not weakness, it's empathy. In fact, all of the traits that you believe are your flaws will come to be your strengths. The things you thought would hold you back will in fact make you stronger, make you better. They will give you a different kind of power and make you a leader that this world, with all its turmoil, might just desperately need.

That is what I would tell her.

And I suppose in sharing my story, that's what I'm telling *you*.

In January 2023, I stood in a hotel room in Napier. It was the start of a new political year. The Labour Party would, as usual, mark this new start with a retreat that would allow us to plan for the year ahead. Clarke, Neve, and I had flown in the night before. We'd arrived late, eaten snacks for dinner, and tried to settle Neve into yet another hotel room.

Clarke was on the far side of the room, dunking a bag of tea into a mug of hot water. Behind him was the unmade bed, our suitcases on the floor. In the adjoining room, I heard Neve bustling about, entertaining herself with quiet chatter.

Neve's head peered round the doorway. "Mummy, I laid out all my teas. I'm ready for a tea party."

I nodded as I picked out my outfit for the day's events. "That sounds fun, my love." Neve disappeared. Clarke handed me my tea. I took a few sips, then set down my mug. I pulled my dress over my head and looked in the mirror to smooth down my hair.

"Feel okay?" Clarke asked.

"I think so." I slid on my shoes and picked up my handbag. By now, I had made my decision, and I was about to announce it. First to my Labour colleagues, and then to the world.

"Wait, Mum!" Neve stood in the doorway. "I thought you were coming to my tea party. Pleeease!"

I peeked into her room. She'd opened all of the packets of tea, removing the sachets and laying them out on her desk, side by side. Yellow chamomile, red English breakfast, green peppermint. Neve had placed the teacups on the desk—the cups beside the saucers instead of on top of them. On each saucer, she carefully placed two shortbread cookies. "Will you play with me?" she asked.

I wrapped my arm around her, kissed her unbrushed hair. *I'd love to,* I murmured. *Just as soon as I get back.*

Less than a week after that visit to Napier, I was back in Wellington, in the rear seat of a ministerial car. Clarke sat next to me, his arm leaning against the passenger window. We'd just dropped off Neve at day care. I pulled out my phone and opened the contact information for John Campbell, the reporter who'd interviewed me on a bright day, nearly five and a half years earlier, when I headed to be sworn in to a job I'd never imagined having.

John didn't answer—busy reporting the news, I imagined—so I decided to leave him a voice memo.

Hey, John, I said. The car was rolling down Featherston Street. *I'm just in the car and on the way to Government House to officially resign.*

Back in Napier, when I'd left Neve and Clarke in the hotel room, I'd walked into a small, unadorned conference room to break the news to my cabinet: I was stepping down. Then I went to the larger, upstairs space, overlooking the sea, where the caucus of party members was assembled, and told them. Then, finally, I held a press conference, and I told the country. Now I was heading to Government House, where a new Labour prime minister, Chris Hipkins, would be sworn in.

I wasn't done. I wasn't done trying to help people, to make the world a little brighter. I'd never be done with those goals. I just wasn't going to do it as prime minister anymore. Following your passion, giving it your all and never giving up, is important, but so is listening to your heart and knowing when it is time to change things, to try a new way, or even to leave.

I continued my note to John:

It felt like nice symmetry to send you a little message. Because of course I was talking to you on the way to become prime minister.

I think you'd asked me what I wanted to be remembered by, and I'm pretty sure I said I wanted to be remembered for kindness.

My voice cracked a little at that last part.

I hope that turned out to be true.

A full ten seconds passed before I could continue. I can still remember, even now, how Clarke turned to me, smiled, and took my hand.

I had not been everyone's first image of a leader, including my own. I was a very ordinary person who found myself in a set of extraordinary circumstances. But I had been a leader. And I had done it on my own terms.

In these final moments as prime minister, the car was passing Queens Wharf. I finished my message to John. *Despite how I sound*, I said, *I'm leaving with nothing but happiness.*

Yes, I realized. I *was* happy. Happiness is a lot of things. And I had found plenty of it in this unexpected job I'd had. But the happiness I felt now came from knowing simply that I had done my best. Whatever the challenge, whatever came at me, I had done my best. And that was enough.

I hung up the phone and looked forward, toward the road in front of us, toward the moments that I still couldn't imagine, toward everything that still lay ahead.

A new era was about to begin.

EPILOGUE

ON ONE OF my school visits about a year into my first term as prime minister, I stood at the front of a school auditorium, looking out at a sea of faces. There were no seats; the kids were all sitting on the floor. I was about to take a tour of the school, but first, I was asked to say a few words to this group of several hundred senior students. I knew that they were about to go into exams.

I hadn't really prepared what I would say, but there was something about this auditorium. I could imagine the exams about to take place: desks spaced out with plastic chairs behind them. Teachers walking up and down the aisles. The feeling that whatever you do in the next few hours will set a path for you, for better or for worse.

A flicker of memory placed me back in my own school auditorium in Morrinsville, where long rows of desks had been set up, and I was sitting at one of them, the pens I had packed in a small Ziploc bag lined up neatly before me. It was the day of the English school certificate exam, one of a series of three-hour exams in each subject area that students have been told over and over are the most important exams of their lives, those that employers and universities will value more highly than any others. I was both exhausted and wired, having barely slept the night before due to nerves, even though I was thoroughly prepared, even though English was one of my best subjects. But when time came for the actual test, I did not pace myself.

"Place your pens down, please."

The last section, the creative writing section, which I had mapped out perfectly for weeks, was left incomplete. A year of work and study, and my grade would come from an exam I didn't even finish. I cried the entire walk home.

"Good morning," I said to the students in the auditorium as I stood up to speak. Some looked at me and murmured hello, others were leaning into their friends. "I have a question for you." A few more heads turned my way. "Who thinks I have a hard job?" A tentative look among the students, a quick glance between one another, and then hands went up, one by one.

"Okay, so most of you. And you'd be right. I do have a hard job. You never know what might happen. At every moment you have to be prepared for a disaster. You need to make big decisions every day, solve problems every day, and manage a team of people who have really hard jobs too.

"And yet," I told them, walking back and forth in front of them, "and yet, for all of that, I wouldn't go back to being sixteen years old again for anything." There was a small rumble of laughter. A few more faces looked in my direction.

"I bet at some point, someone has told you that you are lucky. That being a young person is easy. That you have nothing big to worry about, not compared to what you have to take on as an adult." There were a few nods, a few smiles of recognition. "I don't think that's true. The things you deal with as a young person might be different than the things you'll face as an adult. But that doesn't mean it feels easier."

I thought about Louise getting pinned down and beaten up at school in Murupara and the little boy we saw crying and cold and alone on an icy day. I thought about teenaged Grant, closeted and hurting from isolation and bullying. I thought about Theo. I thought about what the kids in this auditorium face every day, how the world they were growing up in, and the technology they were surrounded by, meant that there was no escape from peer pressure, no release from never-ending reminders of falling short. I told them that I'd made mistakes when I was sixteen that made me feel like my whole world had fallen apart.

"And yet, here I am. That same person, doing hard things and telling you that whether you are young and taking an exam, or a bit older and running the country, it can sometimes feel exactly the same. It can feel really hard."

My eyes landed on a girl. As I finished talking, I saw her looking down, and her face tightened. Her lips were pursed and she squeezed her eyes closed as if she was holding back tears. She rubbed her eyes hard, and when she opened them, she was looking at the floor, blinking a few tears away, determinedly not making eye contact with anyone.

I knew that face.

That, I thought, was me.

"If it feels hard, it's because it is. So please, be kind to yourself. You are not weak, you are human."

I looked at the young people staring back at me.

"And you are enough, just as you are."

Acknowledgments

WHEN THE IDEA of writing a memoir was first presented to me, I wanted to create something that would be meaningful for my fourteen-year-old self. But a book that covers a fifteen-year career in politics isn't the most digestible text for young people. That's why my first thank-you goes to Ruby Shamir for her careful expertise and the passion that went into creating this adaptation.

To Talia and Philomel for the wisdom and patience, and for making this process a joy. To the team at CAA for being a formidable cheer squad. To Ali Benjamin for helping me to become an author in the first place, and for your friendship. To Holly for the endless research and fact-checking, Stacey Morrison for her expertise, and the Alexander Turnbull Library's Political Diary Oral History Project. And to all those who were such an important part of this story—my colleagues, my family, and my friends—thank you.

And finally to Clarke and Neve. I love you. You are my next chapter.

JACINDA ARDERN

was elected prime minister of New Zealand in 2017 at the age of thirty-seven and became the country's youngest prime minister in more than 150 years. Since leaving office, Ardern has established the Field Fellowship on empathetic leadership. She continues to work on climate action and is the patron of the Christchurch Call to Action to eliminate terrorist and violent extremist content online. Ardern also works on a number of projects that support women and girls, but she considers her greatest roles to be those she will hold for life, including that of mum and proud New Zealander.